COCKTAILS
& CANAPES

COCKTAILS & CANAPES

How to throw the very best party, whatever the size

Kathy Kordalis

Hardie Grant

BOOKS

CONTENTS

Why have a cocktail party? All that preparation, all that stress?

Because it is fun! There's nothing like that moment when a cocktail party clicks into gear and bursts into life – guests arriving and exchanging greetings, drinks being poured with a clinking of ice and delicious smells coming from the oven as the first canapés are passed around. This is the moment when a good host can relax and focus on the most important tasks: helping people to mingle, adding positive energy and setting the mood. The key to a party is a relaxed host.

A great party is a feast for all the senses. The ball starts rolling with quality food and drinks, and preparation is required for that. The fun should begin in getting ready for a party, and this book has been written to make sure it can.

Follow these tips on how to cater a party, the number of cocktails and canapés to serve per person, tips on how to plan and prepar and a simple time plan, and you can be that relaxed host.

Searching for the perfect party cocktails? From Frozen Margarita (page 50) to an elegant Pink Champagne Cocktail (page 28), this book has you covered with a round-up of classic and contemporary concoctions.

Nibbles? Read on for a variety of delicious morsels that can be mixed and matched to suit any taste – from comforting Macaroni Cheese Bites with Cayenne Crumb, to super-simple Quail's Eggs with Avocado and Yuzu Whip.

By keeping canapés colourful, flavourful and textured they will satisfy all the senses. Food doesn't need to be complicated; a good quality bowl of crisps and a pimped-up dip is a great place to start. Add a large bowl of olives and some crudités served on beds of ice in an array of glass dishes and you have the beginnings of a gorgeous centrepiece – and no stress.

There's a Dos and Don'ts section (page 14) and some suggestions for menu planners (page 16). There are vodka, gin, whisky, rum, tequila and booze-free cocktail recipes for an eclectic crowd. For food there are sections on everything from simple, pimped-up snacks, to showstopping platters and too pretty to resist desserts, as well as a wealth of free-from options.

Most recipes can be made easier – an element can be bought or substituted if you're pushed for time. Many of the recipes can be made in advance and heated just before serving them, and there are platter suggestions for if you only have time to make a couple of canapés and want more options for a large gathering.

It's all in the planning and prep. Bear these few questions in mind when you're planning the party, and you can't go wrong.

Planning Question List

How many guests are you having?

When you know the number, you can plan how many and which canapés to serve. For a standing-up party at home that will last four hours, 12 canapés per person, a mixture of hot and cold, two of them sweet, is about right, and one or one-and-a-half drinks per hour.

This doesn't mean 12 different types of canapé, just 12 each, and that's assuming that the canapé party is the main event of the evening. If your guests are going on to another event later, or to dinner, six canapés per person will be enough.

Three to six types of canapé should be achievable (depending on how adventurous you're feeling). Always serve a combination of hot and cold and a couple of sweet options. If you're pressed for time, chocolate truffles and coffee always goes down well.

If the party is going to last longer, serve a few extra dips and crudités and a cheeseboard. To cover all bases, include gluten-free, dairy-free and vegan options.

What are the guests' dietary requirements?

Find out if your guests have any allergies or dietary requirements. This is very helpful during the planning stage, as your guests will feel taken care of and you won't get stressed on the night.

How many hours will the party last?

Four hours is a good catering time-gauge, but obviously parties can last longer, and if they do, you will need to have extra food. It's a good idea to have food in the refrigerator that you can easily make a platter of if you need to, but that you can use in meals over the coming week if you don't.

Will people be moving on to a dinner or another event?

As with the time-frame, knowing this will help you decide what to serve. If people are going to be eating more later, you can keep the cocktails and canapés light and easy.

Will you serve just canapés, or sharing platters as well?

Sharing patters are impressive and save time. Deciding what kind to serve will help you choose what canapés to make. Also, you can plan how you will serve it all: a mixture of wooden boards and platters, or on a selection of plates.

Preparation

Start by deciding on your menu. As you do so, think about short-cuts – what you'll make yourself and what you'll buy ready-made. Have vegan, gluten-free and dairy-free options and one or two cocktail options with sparkling water, red and white wine, sparkling wine and beer. It's more than acceptable to ask your friends for help: can they bring a bottle of wine, some cheese, or even a platter? Then you can focus on making the cocktails and canapés.

Shopping List

When you have the numbers, the timings and the menu worked out, it's time to make your shopping list. Start by focusing on the recipes, then add the extras.

Think about having an extra something in the refrigerator such as a simple selection of cheese. It could be a good Cheddar and a vegan cheese, plus some gluten-free crackers and bread, or a selection of dips and corn chips or items for an antipasti platter – or maybe some smoked salmon and cream cheese.

Don't forget ...

- Ice (ever). A party without ice is not a party. Buy a bag or two in advance and keep it in your freezer. If you have limited space, buy it an hour before your friends arrive and keep it in a cool box or supermarket cool bag.
- Cocktail napkins
- Cocktail sticks
- Quality coffee (for a French press)
- Good vanilla ice cream (vegan or not). If you don't have time to make a sweet canapé you can always serve a scoop of ice cream, small coffees and a whisky or dessert wine to finish the night off.

10

Basic Time Plan

This will be your most helpful tool, but it can be as simple as the example below:

Four weeks before
- Make guest list
- Send invites

Two weeks before
- Confirm numbers and dietary requirements
- Plan menu
- Make shopping list
- Book online delivery
- Think about decorating extras; flowers, fruit bowls, crudité centrepieces, pots of herbs, candles and lighting, etc.

One week before
- Start preparation – make and freeze as much as possible

Two days before
- Prep the fresh food that will keep, then cover and chill
- Pull out all your serving dishes and think about the items you'll serve on them

The day before
- Bring out all the decorations and set them up
- Have a final clean and tidy
- Chill the wine, sparkling water and beer
- Finish the food
- It's all good – you've got this!

On the day
- Defrost anything that you've frozen
- Make a final check if you need anything
- Buy ice and anything you might have forgotten
- Line baking trays

An hour before the guests arrive
- Light the candles, mix the cocktails, turn the oven on
- As soon as your first guest arrives, serve drinks and start heating the warm canapés, interspersing with cold options
- Smile, have fun and enjoy the party

Decorating Extras

This is where you can really have fun! You can include bowls of fruit for people to eat and bowls of crudités on ice that can double as centrepieces. Combine vegetables with flowers, such as artichokes on stalks with lovely hydrangeas or decorate simple wine glasses with single flowers. All of these things can be bought from the supermarket – it's just about being creative. A single colour can be super-chic – yellow candles, vases with yellow flowers, glass bowls with lemons, for instance, and then serve your canapés with yellow cocktail napkins, and make a simple lemonade to serve.

If in doubt, ask for help!

Your friends won't mind – if you were a guest, would you? Lots of people put requests on invitations nowadays, such as 'bring a bottle'.

If a friend offers to help out, you could ask them to bring an antipasti platter or some nice bread. Or maybe to come an hour or two early to help assemble canapés, mix cocktails or help answering the door and taking coats. It's all helpful. At the end of the party, if someone offers to wash up, accept!

Recipe Information

Each recipe in the book is accompanied by symbols to indicate what dietary requirements it caters for. In cases where dairy cheese is used recipes are marked as vegetarian, but always check the package carefully to see if animal rennet is used, or look for a vegetarian or vegan alternative.

V	vegetarian
VG	vegan friendly
DF	dairy-free
GF	gluten-free
NF	nut-free

Always use free-range meat, wash herbs and vegetables before use, and assume that eggs, unless otherwise specified, are large.

13

Dos and Don'ts

There are rules and there are helpful guidelines, and these are the latter. Their general purpose is to guide you to plan ahead for minimum fuss and maximum pleasure!

Do

- Think of a theme to inspire your canapé menu – in the festive season, use warming spices and ingredients such as cranberries. Or go Italian with an antipasti platter and a selection of Italian-style canapés to match, with glasses of prosecco.
- Have gluten-free and vegan options; it will make your life easier, and, after all, you are a gracious host!
- With canapés, size matters. They should be no bigger than bite-sized for easy eating, but pack them with flavour by combining sweet, salty, bitter, savoury and sour.
- Make as much as possible ahead and keep fresh canapés and those that need assembling to the last hour. There are many types of canapé that can be made in advance and frozen and reheated just before serving. This will leave you more time to enjoy your own party.
- Think of taste, colour and texture – add crunch by using toast or a crisp vegetable such as cucumber or lettuce as a base for canapés.
- Arrange the canapés on a beautiful platter, tray or board and be sure to serve them with cocktail napkins.
- Have a few extras in the refrigerator in case the party keeps rolling and people stay longer.
- Keep it simple – that's always chicest!
- Plan and prepare – it helps keep things simple.
- Have fun – what's the point otherwise?

Don't

- Go crazy with adornments – just use them to make your canapés pretty and add a bit of flavour. You don't want to create a canapé that's impossible to pick up and pop in your mouth.
- Overcomplicate by setting an unrealistic menu if you're super-busy or short on time.
- Forget to buy ice – no-one wants warm cocktails.
- Put away the bottles that guests bring – add them to the party selection and if you don't drink one, tell the guest who brought it you'll share it with them another time – and do it!
- Forget to have fun. There are more dos than don'ts for a good reason!

Simple menu ideas for all sorts of fabulous parties, whether they are casual, retro or evening soirées. With drink and food options that are both delicious and nice to look at!

Casual Christmas Drinks

Elegant Brunch

Evening Soirée

Pre-party

Lazy Afternoon

Retro Games Night

Menu Planners

COCKTAILS

Cocktails

Gin-based

Cherry Bomb **V, VG, DF, GF**

Pink Hibiscus **V, VG, DF, GF, NF**

Jalapeño Ginger Cooler **V, VG, DF, GF, NF**

Pink Champagne Cocktail **DF, GF, NF**

Vodka-based

Melontini **V, VG, DF, GF, NF**

Pepper & Strawberry Vodka Cocktail **V, VG, DF, GF, NF**

Lime & Honey Vodka Cocktail **V, DF, GF, NF**

Cucumber & Ginger Sparkle **V, VG, DF, GF, NF**

Whisky-based

Mulled Wine with a Dash of Whisky **DF, GF, NF**

Cranberry Spiced Punch **V, VG, DF, GF, NF**

Liquorice Whisky Cocktail **V, VG, DF, GF, NF**

Rum-based

Berry & Basil Daiquiri **V, VG, DF, GF, NF**

Lime & Lemongrass Rum Jug **V, DF, GF, NF**

Classic Piña Colada Jug **V, VG, DF, GF, NF**

Tequila-based

Watermelon Tequila Cocktail **V, VG, DF, GF, NF**

Jasmine Tequila Mojito **V, VG, DF, GF, NF**

Frozen Margarita **V, VG, DF, GF, NF**

Lemon Verbena Tequila **V, VG, DF, GF, NF**

Tequila Sunrise Punch **V, VG, DF, GF, NF**

Make-ahead Infusions

Cucumber & Mint Gin **V, VG, DF, GF, NF**

Dessert Amaretto **V, VG, DF, GF**

Citrus Punch **V, VG, DF, GF, NF**

Peach & Raspberry **V, VG, DF, GF, NF**

Booze-free

Orange Fizz **V, DF, GF, NF**

Muddled Berries with Cloves **V, VG, DF, GF, NF**

Watermelon & Elderflower **V, VG, DF, GF, NF**

Ginsoda **V, VG, DF, GF, NF**

Syrups, Shrubs & Cordials

Strawberry & Rhubarb Cordial **V, VG, DF, GF, NF**

Cranberry & Anise Shrub **V, DF, GF, NF**

Syrups **V, VG, DF, GF, NF**

Cherry Bomb

Menu Planner
Pre-party
(page 18)

The base for this super-elegant cocktail can be made in advance and shaken with ice when your guests arrive – that way you'll get froth on each cocktail. It's worth it!

Makes 1

50 ml (1¾ fl oz/3 tablespoons) gin
20 ml (1½ tablespoons) cherry syrup
30 ml (2¼ tablespoons) grapefruit juice
30 ml (2¼ tablespoons) lemon juice
30 ml (2¼ tablespoons) aquafaba (liquid from a can of cooked chickpeas)

TO SERVE
sprig of thyme

Combine all the ingredients in a cocktail shaker with a few ice cubes. Put the lid on and shake well until super-frothy, about 30–40 seconds. Strain into a glass and garnish with a sprig of thyme.

| V | VG | DF | GF |

Gin-based

Pink Hibiscus

This pretty combination is sure to impress! It also can quite easily be a non-alcoholic drink – just omit the gin or use alcohol-free gin. This has the mild, tangy, cranberry-like tannin undertones of hibiscus tea and a pretty, preserved hibiscus flower.

Serves 4–6

400 ml (13 fl oz/generous 1½ cups) hibiscus tea, cooled
300 ml (10 fl oz/1¼ cups) gin
150 ml (5 fl oz/scant ⅔ cup) pink grapefruit juice
1 tablespoon Rose syrup (page 68)
Soda water (optional)

TO SERVE
Hibiscus flowers in syrup

Mix the hibiscus tea, gin, grapefruit juice and Rose syrup in a jug. Add ice and serve strained into cocktail glasses garnished with a hibiscus flower in each. Alternatively, serve in a jug with the ice, topped with soda water.

| **V** | **VG** | **DF** | **GF** | **NF** |

26

Jalapeño Ginger Cooler

This is a fresh and spicy cocktail that can be made in advance and just topped up with diet ginger beer.

Serves 8

300ml (10 fl oz/1¼ cups) gin
1–2 jalapeños, chopped
   (depending on heat)
1 long cucumber
1 thumb-sized piece fresh ginger
   root, peeled and grated
100 ml (3½ fl oz/scant ½ cup)
   Cointreau
100 ml (3½ fl oz/scant ½ cup)
   lime juice
diet ginger beer

Infuse the gin with the chopped jalapeño for 30–45 minutes or until you can taste the heat of the chilli. Meanwhile, blitz the cucumber with the grated ginger in a food processor and pass through a sieve to remove the pulp, pressing gently with a spatula to extract as much juice as possible.

Half fill a large jug with ice. Pour in the jalapeño-infused gin and the cucumber and ginger juice, followed by the Cointreau and lime juice, and top with the ginger beer. Mix well.

| V | VG | DF | GF | NF |

Gin-based

Pink Champagne Cocktail

Simplicity at its best. These can quite easily be made with your favourite juice or fruit purée instead of the lemonade. In summer I love using tropical fruit purées with a squeeze of lime.

Serves 8

250 ml (8½ fl oz) gin
250 ml (8½ fl oz)
  pink lemonade
1 bottle Champagne

Divide the gin and pink lemonade between eight Champagne flutes. Top up each glass with Champagne.

Serving Tip

These look lovely served on a tray. Champagne should always be served very chilled, so by placing the glasses in the refrigerator an hour before your guests arrival will ensure that the drink is cold.

Menu Planner
Elegant
Brunch
(*page 17*)

| DF | GF | NF |

Melontini

This drink is summer in a glass, with the melon balls emitting a sweet aroma. Freeze the melon balls in advance and pop them into glasses when your guests arrive.

Serves 8

400 ml (13 fl oz/generous
  1½ cups) vodka
100 ml (3½ fl oz/scant ½ cup)
  melon liqueur
2–3 tablespoons sugar syrup
  (simple syrup), to taste
2 limes, juiced

TO SERVE
1 melon, made into balls
  (see introduction)
mini kiwi fruit, sliced

Mix the vodka, melon liqueur, syrup and lime juice in a jug or bottle and allow the flavours to meld for at least 4 hours.

Fill glasses with ice and divide the mixture, melon balls and mini kiwi fruit between them.

Serving Tip
If you are pressed for time, balling the melon might seem like a faff. If that's the case, simply blitz the melon into a puree and add is as a liquid, It will make the mixture thicker, but still as delicious!

| **V** | **VG** | **DF** | **GF** | **NF** |

Pepper & Strawberry Vodka Cocktail

These pretty cocktails are sweet and hot, with a black pepper kick that will liven up your do. In summer, I add a well-cleaned daisy flower head.

Serves 8

650 ml (21¾ fl oz/
   2¾ cups) vodka
300 g (10½ oz)
   strawberries, cut
   lengthways, leaves
   intact
50 ml (3 tablespoons)
   sugar syrup (simple
   syrup)
1 tablespoon black
   peppercorns
daisy flower heads,
   cleaned and dried
   (optional)

Mix the ingredients and allow to infuse for a minimum of 24 hours (48 is better). When ready to serve, sieve, reserving the strawberries.

To serve, drop an ice cube into each glass, pour in the infusion and top with a reserved strawberry, and a daisy flower head, if using.

Serving Tip

If you have time, you can set the reserved strawberries and daisy heads in ice to serve.

| V | VG | DF | GF | NF |

Vodka-based

Lime & Honey Vodka Cocktail

Menu Planner
Evening
Soirée
(*page 18*)

This cocktail is great served chilled in summer, or served warm in winter. If you're feeling under the weather, or your soul needs a boost, just heat gently in a saucepan but don't let it boil.

Serves 6–8

600 ml (20 fl oz/2½ cups) vodka
4 limes, juiced
60 ml (2 fl oz/¼ cup) clear
  blossom honey

TO SERVE
soda water (optional)
strips of lime zest (optional)

Mix all the ingredients in a jug and chill until ready to serve. Ten minutes before you serve, add some ice to the jug and keep in the refrigerator. Serve either neat in cocktail glasses, or add soda water and serve on ice in highball glasses, both garnished with strips of lime zest.

| V | | DF | GF | NF |

34

Cucumber & Ginger Sparkle

Refreshing, vivacious, light and easy to share with a crowd. This is the simplest of combinations, adding cucumber to make this fizzy vodka tipple and ginger beer creates elegance. Low sugar ginger beer is great alternative to the sugar laden ones.

Serves 6–8

2 cucumbers, thinly sliced
   lengthways
3 limes, cut into thin wedges
handful of mint leaves, torn
3 tablespoons sugar syrup (simple
   syrup)
300 ml (10 fl oz/1¼ cups) vodka
ginger beer

Divide the cucumbers, limes and mint between glasses. Mix the sugar syrup and vodka together in a jug. Divide equally between the glasses and muddle to infuse the flavours. Top with ice and some ginger beer to add the sparkle.

| V | VG | DF | GF | NF |

35

Mulled Wine
with a Dash of Whisky

Nothing beats a traditional mulled wine, gently simmering and filling the your home with those comforting aromas. For a tipple with an extra little something, add a dash of whisky. It feels so grown-up.

Serves 8–10

2 bottles medium-bodied red wine
1 thumb-sized piece fresh ginger
   root, peeled and sliced
1 orange, halved and squeezed
   (squeezed halves retained)
3 cinnamon sticks
12 cloves
3 cardamom pods, bruised
3 tablespoons honey (or to taste)
whisky, to top up each glass

Combine all of the ingredients, including the squeezed orange halves, in a saucepan and heat to just simmering. Continue barely simmering, covered, for at least 30 minutes. Taste and adjust. Drink with a dash of whisky added to each glass.

Serving Tip
Serve in nice mugs or teacups to help keep the mixture warm.

| DF | GF | NF |

37

COCKTAILS & CANAPES

Cranberry Spiced Punch

Menu Planner
Casual Christmas Drinks
(page 17)

This chilled festive punch is great to share and a nice change from the warm one. Serve it on ice with fresh, tangy cranberries that pop when you bite into them. To add some extra elements, you can also mix in orange juice, fresh orange slices and some prosecco.

Serves 6–8

400 ml (13 fl oz/generous 1½ cups) whisky
1 litre (34 fl oz/4 cups) cranberry juice
3 tablespoons vanilla essence
3 tablespoons maple syrup
200 g (7 oz) fresh cranberries

TO SERVE
6–8 cinnamon sticks

Mix the whisky, cranberry juice, vanilla essence, maple syrup, fresh cranberries and some ice in a jug or punch bowl.

Serve in cups or glasses with extra ice, some of the fresh cranberries and cinnamon sticks.

Serving Tip
These are so much fun served in earthenware mugs or stoneware cups. If you can't find fresh cranberries, infuse 150 g (5½ oz) dried cranberries in the whisky overnight, which will infuse the whisky and the cranberries when you serve them.

| V | VG | DF | GF | NF |

Whisky-based

Liquorice Whisky Cocktail

Neat and simply sexy. An intriguing pairing of liquorice and whisky, this drink is all about the subtlety of flavours. The warm and savoury notes of the liquorice complement the whisky to create an interesting twist. This can easily be multiplied by the number of guests you are serving.

Makes 1

50 ml (1¾ fl oz/3 tablespoons) whisky
dash of liquorice syrup (a little goes a long way)
8 fresh liquorice sticks or a good quality liquorice, to garnish
dash of soda water (optional)

Serve a single measure of whisky and a dash of liquorice syrup over ice with a liquorice garnish. Add a dash of soda water to give it some fizz, if you like.

| V | VG | DF | GF | NF |

40

Berry & Basil Daiquiri

A summer holiday in a glass. This recipe uses basil, which marries nicely with berries, but could be just as delicious with mint. As its a frozen drink, it needs to be drunk as soon as you blitz it ... don't let it sit around.

Serves 8

150 ml (5 fl oz/⅔ cup) white rum
6 basil leaves
500 g (1 lb 2 oz) frozen mixed
   raspberries and strawberries
agave nectar, to taste
sparkling water (optional)

TO SERVE
strawberries
basil sprigs

Place the rum, basil and berries in a food processor and blitz to a smooth purée. Taste to determine the sweetness balance. Depending on how sweet your berries are, add a little agave nectar to balance and serve in cocktail glasses and garnish with basil and fresh strawberries.

Serve in cocktail glasses garnished with basil and strawberries.

Serving Tip
This is also delicious served in a highball glass with a dash of sparkling water.

| V | VG | DF | GF | NF |

Lime & Lemongrass Rum Jug

Menu Planner
Lazy Afternoon
(page 19)

Bring the tropics into your home with this recipe. Perfect for a summer barbecue, a lazy brunch or a get-together with friends when you want minimum fuss and maximum fun.

Serves 4

200 ml (7 fl oz/scant 1 cup)
   white rum
2 lemongrass stalks, bruised
3 limes, cut into wedges
1–2 tablespoons clear runny honey
   (or to taste)
2–3 lime leaves (optional)
ice cubes
soda water, to taste

TO SERVE
1 lime, halved widthways
bee pollen

Put the rum in a jug with the lemongrass stalks and allow to infuse for at least 30 minutes, or overnight, in the refrigerator.

When ready to serve add the lime wedges, runny honey and lime leaves (if using) and muddle in the jug. Add ice and soda water.

To serve, rub lime around the rims of the glasses then dip the rims into the bee pollen. Allow the bee pollen to dry before filling the glasses.

| **V** | | **DF** | **GF** | **NF** |

Rum-based

Classic Piña Colada

Sunshine, sandy beaches and the scent of pineapple and coconut. The revival of this retro cocktail is perfect for a canapé party. For a twist, infuse with lime leaves and garnish with shop-bought dehydrated limes. Or the traditional way of serving a Piña Colada, garnished with a fresh slice of pineapple and a marachino cherry.

Serves 8

500 ml (17 fl oz/2 cups) pineapple juice
250 ml (8½ fl oz/1 cup) white rum
250 ml (8½ fl oz/1 cup) coconut cream
crushed ice

TO SERVE
8 slices of pineapple
8 maraschino cherries

Whizz the pineapple juice, rum, coconut cream and a small handful of crushed ice together in a blender.

Pour into glasses and garnish with pineapple and cherries.

Serving Tip
Jazz it up by adding some umbrellas!

| V | VG | DF | GF | NF |

Rum-based

Watermelon Tequila

The union of watermelon, tequila and cayenne pepper makes for a simply great drink.
Sweet and spicy and finished with a cooling little wedge of watermelon.

Serves 6

1 small watermelon
200 ml (7 fl oz/scant 1 cup) blanco
   (silver) tequila
cayenne pepper
agave syrup
dash of Angostura bitters
1 lime, juiced

Remove the skin and roughly chop the watermelon, reserve some for garnish, then remove the seeds from the rest and put it in a food processor. Add the tequila, blitz, and pour into a jug or jar and, tasting as you go, add cayenne pepper, agave syrup, Angostura bitters and the lime.

Serve in little glasses with wedges of watermelon and a sprinkling of cayenne for extra kick.

| V | VG | DF | GF | NF |

Jasmine Tequila Mojito

For the best results, start this the day before. The scented jasmine tea is infused and the mixture is frozen overnight then muddled into your Mojito. The addition of the jasmine with its subtle sweetness and fragrance makes for an interesting take.

Serves 6

2 jasmine tea bags
500 ml (20 fl oz/2 cups) boiling water
3 limes, sliced
½ bunch mint leaves
2–3 tablespoons agave syrup
200 ml (7 fl oz/scant 1 cup) blanco (silver) tequila

Make the jasmine tea in a jug with the boiling water and allow to cool. Once cooled, discard the tea bags, pour the liquid into ice trays and freeze overnight.

To make the mojitos, muddle the limes with the mint and agave, pour into tall glasses, add the jasmine tea ice cubes and pour over the tequila, stirring as you go.

| V | VG | DF | GF | NF |

Tequila-based

Frozen Margarita

This is so much fun but yet so simple and impressive. For best results, make this mixture overnight and freeze in a container and blitz just as your friends arrive!

Serves 6

200 ml (7 fl oz/scant 1 cup) fresh lime juice
400 ml (13 fl oz/ generous 1½ cups) blanco (silver) tequila
200 ml (7 fl oz/scant 1 cup) Triple Sec
300 ml (10 fl oz/ 1¼ cups) water
150 ml (5 fl oz/scant ⅔ cup) agave syrup

TO SERVE
400–550 g (14–18 oz/3–4 cups) ice cubes
lime wedges
Himalayan fine sea salt (optional)

Mix all the ingredients together and freeze overnight in a plastic container.

When ready to serve, put the frozen margarita mixture into a high-powered blender and blend to the texture of a slushy. Add ice and blend until smooth.

Serving Tip
Rim some margarita glasses with salt, if you like, and serve with lime wedges.

Menu Planner
Retro Games Night
(*page 50*)

| V | VG | DF | GF | NF |

50

Lemon Verbena Tequila

The simple lemon verbena herb packs a real flavour punch! Its strong lemon-lime flavour also has a fruity aroma, which infuses perfectly with tequila. Great to have on hand for shots, should the occasion arise.

Makes 700 ml (23½ fl oz)

4 lemon verbena sprigs
1 tablespoon agave nectar
700 ml (23½ fl oz) tequila

TO SERVE
fine sea salt
lime wedges

Put the lemon verbena and simple syrup in a sterilised 1 litre (34 fl oz) glass jar or bottle and pour over the tequila. Seal the jar tightly and store in a cool, dark place for 3 days, gently shaking the jar occasionally to help infuse the flavours.

Strain the tequila through a fine-mesh sieve into a large jug, and discard the herbs. Strain again through a fine-mesh sieve lined with muslin (cheesecloth) or a coffee filter. Transfer to one large or several smaller sterilised glass bottles and seal tightly. Serve with salt and wedges of lime.

| V | VG | DF | GF | NF |

Tequila Sunrise Punch

This is sure will get the party started. This classic 1970s cocktail has been turned into a punch with layers of sliced oranges, pineapple juice and Tequila.

Serves 6–8

300 ml (10 fl oz/1¼ cups) blanco (silver) tequila
500 ml (17 fl oz/2 cups) orange juice
250 ml (8½ fl oz/1 cup) pineapple juice
200 ml (7 fl oz/scant 1 cup) grenadine syrup
1 bottle Champagne

TO SERVE
orange slices
ice cubes
maraschino cherries

In a punchbowl or large glass jug, layer orange slices with ice. Add tequila, orange juice, pineapple juice, grenadine syrup and Champagne.

Serve garnished with more slices of orange and marashino cherries on toothpicks.

| V | VG | DF | GF | NF |

53

Cucumber & Mint Gin

This recipe is best started 48–72 hours hours in advance. Keep it chilled in the refrigerator and serve on ice and topped up with sparkling water. Or, for a twist, serve with pickled ginger and slices of fresh cucumber.

Serves 10

500 ml (17 fl oz/2 cups) gin
2 cucumbers, sliced into thin rounds
½ bunch mint
2–3 tablespoons ginger syrup
1 lime, juiced

TO SERVE
1 small cucumber, thinly sliced
mint sprigs
pickled ginger
sparkling water

Put all the ingredients in a sterilised jar and store in the refrigerator for 72 hours ideally, or a minimum of 24. Gently shake the jar from time to time to help infuse the flavours.

When ready to serve, strain through a fine-mesh sieve into a large jug, and discard the solids.

Serve it 50 ml (1¾ fl oz/3 tablespoons) per glass, with cucumber, mint, pickled ginger, ice and soda water.

Serving Tip

This recipe is so versatile as it also works perfectly as a jug to share! Just add the infused gin to a jug with ice and top up with a mixture if sparkling water and low sugar ginger beer. Add a final garnish of fresh cucumber, mint leaves muddle and serve in tumbers.

| **V** | **VG** | **DF** | **GF** | **NF** |

55

Dessert Amaretto

Menu Planner
Evening Soirée
(page 18)

This is the most satisfying infusion to make; the humblest of ingredients achieve such a lovely result. It will take a few days, but it's worth it. Serve it in a little, fine glass with a tray of chocolate truffles. Or over a scoop of vanilla ice cream with a shot of espresso.

Serves 10

200 g (7 oz) dark brown sugar
1–2 tablespoons almond extract
2 teaspoons vanilla extract
155 g (5 oz) raw almonds
600 ml (20 fl oz/2½ cups) gin

Combine the dark brown sugar with 250 ml (8½ fl oz/1 cup) water in a saucepan over a medium heat and simmer until the sugar has dissolved. Allow to cool and add the almond extract, vanilla extract, raw almonds and gin and pour into a sterilised jar. Store in cool, dark place for a minimum of 3–5 days, occasionally shaking the jar gently to help infuse the flavours.

Strain the amaretto through a fine-mesh sieve and discard the almonds. Transfer into one large or several smaller sterilised glass bottles.

Serving Tip
Serve a single measure with a tray of chocolate truffles at the end of a meal.

V | VG | DF | GF

Citrus Punch

Menu Planner
Lazy Afternoon
(*page 19*)

A perfect crowd-pleasing drink. Whether you serve it in a punch bowl or in a large jug it is just the same light hearted pleasure.

Serves 10–12

800 ml (28 fl oz/generous 3 cups) vodka
300 ml (10 fl oz/1¼ cups) Aperol
100 ml (3½ fl oz/scant ½ cup) Galliano
200 ml (7 fl oz/scant 1 cup) lime juice
200 ml (7 fl oz/scant 1 cup) pink grapefruit juice

TO SERVE
ice cubes
mixed citrus fruit

Mix all of the ingredients in a jug and chill in the refrigerator for 2–3 days.

When ready to serve, pour into a punch bowl or 2–3 jugs, adding ice cubes and citrus slices.

| V | VG | DF | GF | NF |

58

Peach & Raspberry

This infusion is incredibly refreshing! The tartness of peach and raspberry, when paired with the mustard-like flavour of horseradish, brings out the sweetness of the fruit.

Serves 8–10

600 ml (20 fl oz/2½ cups) gin
2 peaches, cut into wedges
100 g (3½ oz) raspberries
5 cm (2 in) piece horseradish, peeled and grated
agave syrup (to taste)

TO SERVE
soda water
2 peaches, thinly sliced
frozen raspberries, threaded onto cocktail sticks
grated or shredded fresh horseradish

Combine all the ingredients except the agave syrup in a jug or glass bottle and store in the refrigerator for up to 3 days, or until the colour has deepened. Strain the mixture through a sieve, discard the solids and taste – at this point, add as much agave as you need to achieve a balanced flavour. Transfer to a jug.

Divide between glasses and top with soda water, then add the peaches, raspberries and grated horseradish.

| V | VG | DF | GF | NF |

59

Orange Fizz

An elegant and invigorating drink. This is definitely an energy booster and a great booze-free alternative.

Serves 6

2 oranges, juiced
1 lime, juiced
1–2 tablespoons clear runny honey
1–2 teaspoons orange blossom
    extract (or to taste)

TO SERVE
750ml (25 fl oz/3 cups) sparkling
    water
1 orange, sliced

Combine the orange and lime juices, the honey and orange blossom extract to taste. Chill in the refrigerator for a minimum of 30 minutes.

Pour into a jug filled with ice and top with sparkling water and orange slices.

Serving Tip
For those that need an extra kick, add some vodka and half a red chilli to the jug, give it a stir and serve.

| V | | DF | GF | NF |

Muddled Berries
with Cloves

This is a great drink to serve during the festive season. To keep your party fuss-free, serve it in jugs with some gin alongside, so those who fancy a stronger tipple can add a dash if they like.

Serves 6

1–2 tablespoons maple syrup
8 cloves
200 g (7 oz) frozen mixed berries
1 teaspoon vanilla paste

TO SERVE
750 ml (25 fl oz/3 cups) sparkling
  water

Put the maple syrup in a small bowl with the cloves and gently muddle. Leave overnight to infuse, then discard the cloves.

Discard the cloves and, to serve, muddle the berries in the bottom of a jug with the vanilla paste, add the clove-infused maple syrup and top with sparkling water and serve.

Serving Tip
For a fun touch you can serve this with individual bottles of gin as a gift for your guests – they can decide to spike their own drinks or take their bottles home.

| **V** | **VG** | **DF** | **GF** | **NF** |

Orange Fizz, *page 60*
Muddled Berries with Cloves, *page 61*

Watermelon & Elderflower

Menu Planner
Elegant Brunch
(page 17)

Similar to lemonade but with watermelon and elderflower instead. It's booze-free, gentle and fragrant, and perfect for a brunch table. In summer, I make a large jug and keep it in the refrigerator to drink throughout the day.

Serves 4–6

200 g (7 oz) watermelon, sliced into wedges
1–2 limes, juiced
100 ml (3½ fl oz/scant ½ cup) elderflower cordial
½ bunch mint
750 ml (25 fl oz/3 cups) soda or sparkling water

Put the watermelon, lime juice, elderflower cordial, mint and soda in a jug, then gently stir and allow guests to help themselves.

Serving Tip

Serve the jug along side highball glasses three quarters full of ice and topped with a slice of watermelon. During elderflower season, topping each glass with fresh elderflowers is also a great touch.

| **V** | **VG** | **DF** | **GF** | **NF** |

Ginsoda

Alcohol-free gins are absolutely brilliant and you would not even know that you were not having the real thing. My friend and I came up with this as a lower-calorie alternative to your usual sugar-laden gin and tonic. Half tonic and half soda – every little helps.

Menu Planner
Pre-party
(page 18)

Serves 10

500 ml (17 fl oz/2 cups
  alcohol-free gin
150 ml (17 fl oz/2 cups Blackberry
  & Thyme syrup (see page 68)

TO SERVE
ice cubes
3 lemons, cut into thin wedges
300 ml (10½ fl oz/1½ cups) tonic
  water
300 ml (10½ fl oz/1½ cups) soda
  water
sprigs of lemon thyme

Pour the alcohol-free gin and Blackberry & Thyme syrup into a jug and mix well.

Pour into large wine glasses with ice and lemon wedges, topped with the tonic and soda waters and garnished with sprigs of lemon thyme.

Serving Tip

This is lovely served in a large wine glass as mentioned earlier. Or another fun way way is to premake it and serve in vintage soda bottles dotted around the table with garnishes on the side for people to DIY.

| V | VG | DF | GF | NF |

Strawberry & Rhubarb Cordial

Add a dash or two of this cordial to jazz up any drink, alcoholic or not. It's also good stirred through shop-bought vanilla ice-cream to create a ripple effect, refrozen, then served with crushed meringues.

Makes 4–6

450 g (1 lb) rhubarb, cut into small pieces
250 g (9 oz) punnet strawberries, trimmed and hulled
200g (7 oz) caster (superfine) sugar

Heat oven to 200°C (400°F/gas 6).

Put all the ingredients in a baking tray, cover with foil and bake for 20 minutes.

Spoon the fruit into a muslin-lined sieve over a bowl and let it drip for more than an hour before squeezing to remove the liquid. Store it in an airtight bottle in the refrigerator for up to 2 weeks.

Menu Planner
Retro Game
(page 19)

| V | VG | DF | GF | NF |

66

Cranberry & Anise Shrub

This shrub is a concentrated syrup that combines fruit, sugar and vinegar. As a sweet, acidic mixer it can be enjoyed on its own or used in a variety of mixed drinks. This is perfect with vodka and loads of ice.

Makes 4–6

300 g (10½ oz) cranberries
50 g (2 oz) raw honey
7 ml (1½ teaspoons) cider vinegar
4 cloves
3 star anise

Put the cranberries in a sterilised jar and lightly crush with a muddler. Stir in the honey, vinegar and cloves. Store in the refrigerator to infuse for 3 days, then strain through a sieve and serve straight away.

Serving Tip

Try the same base mix with two sliced apples and a handful of fennel fronds , instead of cranberries and spices (pictured).

| V | | DF | GF | NF |

Syrups

These syrups are very versatile whether you use them in cocktails, add them to dressings or drizzle them on desserts. So simple to make and keep in your refrigerator – just in case.

Rose

Makes 400 ml (14 fl oz/1¾ cups)

100 g (3½ oz) caster (superfine) sugar
1–2 tablespoons rosewater
1 teaspoon dried rose petals

Combine 250 ml (8½ fl oz/1 cup) boiling water and sugar in a small saucepan over a low heat and stir until the sugar has dissolved. Remove from the heat, add the rosewater and rose petals and leave to cool completely. Strain the syrup through a sieve, discarding the rose petals. Store in a sterilised bottle in the refrigerator for up to a month.

Blackberry & Thyme

Makes 400 ml (14 fl oz/1¾ cups)

100 g (3½ oz) caster (superfine) sugar
200 g (7 oz) blackberries
5 thyme sprigs

Combine 250 ml (8½ fl oz/1 cup) boiling water and the sugar in a small saucepan and gently stir until the sugar has dissolved. Remove from the heat, add the blackberries and thyme and leave to cool completely. Strain through a sieve, discard the blackberries and thyme and store in the refrigerator for up to a month.

| **V** | **VG** | **DF** | **GF** | **NF** |

68

CANAPES

Snacks

Pecorino & Pancetta Dates **GF, NF**

Smoky Maple Nuts **V, VG, DF, GF**

Sicilian-style Baked Olives **V, VG, DF, GF, NF**

Lime Brown Butter Popcorn **V, VG, GF**

Crispy Potato Skins **V, VG, DF, GF, NF**

Cheesy

Stilton & Ale Rarebit **V, NF**

Macaroni Cheese Bites **V, NF**

Ricotta & Caponata **V**

Feta & Mint Hummus **V, GF, NF**

Halloumi Filo Swirls with Skordalia **V, NF**

Vegetarian

Quail's Eggs with Avocado & Yuzu Whip
V, GF, NF

Wild Mushroom Tartlets **V, NF**

Root Vegetable & Sage Fritters **V, NF**

Potsticker Dumplings **V, VG, DF**

Crispy Tofu with Watercress Dipping Sauce
V, VG, DF, NF

Free-from

Sausage Rolls with Harissa Salsa **V, VG, DF, GF**

Rainbow Fresh Spring Rolls with Spicy Peach Dressing **V, VG, DF, GF**

Sweet Potato Pies with Mango Salsa **V, DF, GF, NF**

Broccoli Spears with Walnut Babaganoush **V, VG, DF, GF**

Vegan Mushroom and Port Pâté with Crunchy Crackers **V, VG, DF**

Polenta Squares with Roasted Cherry Tomatoes **V, GF, NF**

Meat & Seafood

Five Spice Duck Pancakes with Plum Sauce **DF, NF**

Chicken, Artichoke & Olive Pâté **NF**

Thai Meatballs with Coriander Dressing **DF, NF**

Date & Pomegranate Chicken Wings **DF, GF**

Korean Ssam Chicken Skewers **DF, GF, NF**

Mini Schnitzels **GF, NF**

Prawn Cocktail Cups **DF, GF, NF**

Smoked Trout Blinis **NF**

Keralan-style Prawns **DF, GF, NF**

Canapés

Gin & Honey Gravadlax **NF**

Smoked Mackerel Pâté **DF**

Mini Yorkshires with Herb & Horseradish Mayonnaise **NF**

Chorizo & Goat's Cheese Palmiers **NF**

Mini Meat Pies with Bloody Mary Ketchup **NF**

Gochujang Pork with Quick Pickled Carrots **DF, NF**

Lamb and Feta stuffed Gozleme with Muhammara

Platters

Cheesy Pull-apart Bread with Antipasti Board **V**

Mezze Platter **V**

Vegan Platter **V, VG, DF, NF**

Mexican Layer Dip **V, GF, NF**

Roast Chicken Platter **GF**

Desserts

Cheesecake Bites **V, NF**

Mini Cranberry Brownies **V, NF**

Coconut Macaroons **V, GF**

Vegan Truffles **V, VG, DF, GF**

Strawberries Two Ways **V, GF, NF**

Pecorino & Pancetta Dates

Menu Planner
Evening
Soirée
(page 18)

These little morsels are really easy to make and a wonderful blend of sweet and salty. They can be made up to two days in advance and kept on a tray in the refrigerator ready to put in the oven when your friends arrive – the perfect start to any celebration!

Serves 8

20 pieces pecorino or other hard
    cheese
20 medjool dates, slit lengthways
    and pitted
20 sage leaves
10 thin slices of pancetta (cut in half)

TO SERVE
2 tablespoons honey
1 pinch chilli flakes (optional)

Heat the oven to 180°C (350°F/gas 4).

Insert a piece of cheese into each date, followed by a sage leaf, then wrap each date with 1 piece of pancetta, securing it with a toothpick. Arrange the dates 2.5 cm (1 in) apart on a lined baking sheet. Bake for 5 minutes. Turn the dates over. Continue baking until the pancetta is crisp, a few minutes longer.

Transfer to a serving platter, drizzle with honey and finish with chilli flakes, if you like.

GF | **NF**

Smoky Maple Nuts

This is where you can have some fun! You can make these nuts spicier, add citrus or freshen them up with more herbs and use whatever combination of nuts you like. In the festive season I like to make double this recipe and have them on-hand when friends pop round. Gently heat and serve them warm to further enhance the flavours.

Serves 8

100 g (3½ oz/1 cup) pecans
50 g (2 oz/⅓ cup) macadamias
100 g (3½ oz/⅔ cup) cashews
100 g (3½ oz/⅔ cup) almonds
6 tablespoons maple syrup
3 sprigs rosemary, leaves picked and chopped
1 tablespoon dried oregano
2 teaspoons sea salt
1 teaspoon freshly ground black pepper
1–2 teaspoons smoked paprika (depending on how hot it is)
1 pinch of chilli flakes

Heat the oven to 180°C (350°F/gas 4). Line a baking sheet with baking parchment. Put the nuts on the baking sheet and roast for 3 minutes.

Take the tray out of the oven, drizzle over the maple syrup and sprinkle over the rosemary, oregano, sea salt, black pepper, paprika and chilli flakes.

Mix well and return to the oven for another 5–7 minutes, until golden brown. Set aside to cool, then tip into a bowl to serve.

V | VG | DF | GF

Smoky Maple Nuts, *page 77*
Sicilian-style Baked Olives, *page 80*
Lime Brown Butter Popcorn, *page 81*

Sicilian-style Baked Olives

Menu Planner
Pre-party
(page 18)

Olives are a powerhouse of flavour – served with an aperitif or cocktail, they are the perfect way to satisfy the tastebuds and get the party started. These have all the great flavours of Sicily and are finished with fresh herbs, citrus and olive oil.

Serves 8

400 g (14 oz/2¼ cups) mixed green and black olives
3 tablespoons extra virgin olive oil
2 tablespoons balsamic vinegar
1 teaspoon freshly ground black pepper
6 fresh bay leaves
4 garlic cloves, unpeeled, bruised
2 teaspoons herbes de Provence, lightly crushed
1 lemon, thinly sliced into half moons

TO SERVE
1 orange or clementine, halved
1 tablespoon chopped flat-leaf parsley
1 tablespoon chopped mint leaves
1 tablespoon olive oil

Heat the oven to 180°C (350°F/gas 4).

Combine all ingredients, other than those in the 'To Serve' section of the recipe, and put on a lined baking tray. Bake for 15–20 minutes.

Take out of the oven and put in a large bowl, with all the pan juices, and squeeze the orange or clementine into the olives. Allow to cool and finish with the herbs. Serve immediately, or keep in an airtight container in the refrigerator for up to 2 weeks.

Serving Tip
To make it easy for people to nibble, use pitted olives – then there's no need for an extra bowl for pits.

| V | VG | DF | GF | NF |

Lime Brown Butter Popcorn

Menu Planner
Lazy Afternoon
(page 19)

This is definitely posh popcorn with the addition of nutty zing from the drizzle of lime brown butter. Brown butter is cooked to the point where the solids will look very dark, nut brown in colour, and it will smell super toasty. When the lime is added to the butter and finished with Parmesan the popcorn is on another level. You can also add raw peanuts in their skins while popping the corn as an extra touch.

Serves 8

100 g (3½ oz/generous ⅔ cup) popping corn
handful of raw, shelled peanuts (optional)
2 tablespoons rapeseed (canola) oil
pinch of salt

FOR THE LIME BROWN BUTTER
50 g (2 oz/scant ¼ cup) unsalted butter
½ lime, juiced (add another half if you want it super-zingy)
20 g (¾ oz/scant ¼ cup) Parmesan (or vegetarian/vegan alternative), grated

Put the popping corn, peanuts (if using) and oil into a large pan on a medium heat and cover with a lid. Once most of the corn has popped, 2–3 minutes, and the popping sounds are about 3 seconds apart, take the pan off the heat. Add the salt and toss to coat.

For the lime brown butter, in a frying pan on a medium heat, cook the butter for 4–5 minutes until melted and the butter has turned a deep nut-brown colour, swirling the pan often. Season to taste and add the lime juice.

Drizzle over the popcorn, add the grated Parmesan, and serve.

Serving Tip
Cheat by drizzling shop-bought popcorn with the butter, but make sure you taste the popcorn before adding salt.

V | **VG** | **GF**

Crispy Potato Skins

with Vegan Chive Dip

Menu Planner
Retro
Games
Night
(*page 19*)

So so simple, and the simplest things are best. This is such a crowd-pleaser and easy to share. Save the mash from the potatoes to freeze for use in another meal.

Serves 8

8 unpeeled potatoes
4 tablespoons olive oil
sea salt and freshly ground black pepper
1 tablespoon chopped rosemary leaves
1 tablespoon thyme leaves
1 tablespoon dried oregano

VEGAN CHIVE DIP
200 g (7 oz/generous ¾ cup) plant-based yoghurt
1–2 tablespoons olive oil
1 avocado, peeled and stoned, cut into chunks
½ bunch chives, chopped (some reserved for garnish)
1 lime, squeezed
1–2 garlic cloves (depending on size), crushed
sea salt and freshly ground black pepper

Heat the oven to 200°C (400°F/gas 6).

Prick each potato all over and rub with half of the oil. Place them directly on the oven shelf and bake for 50–55 minutes until they feel slightly soft when squeezed, then leave to cool.

Cut each potato lengthways in half and then into quarters. Scoop out the flesh, leaving a layer of potato 1 cm (½ in) thick on the skin.

Brush all over with the remaining oil and arrange in a single layer, skin-side down, on a wire rack in a roasting tin.

Season generously and sprinkle over the rosemary, thyme and oregano.

Bake for 15–20 minutes, turning halfway through, until crisp and golden brown.

To make the dip, blitz the yoghurt, the olive oil, avocado, chives, lime juice and garlic in a food processor. Season with salt and pepper, put in a serving bowl and scatter with the reserved chives.

Serve the potato skins hot, with the vegan chive dip.

| V | VG | DF | GF | NF |

Stilton & Ale Rarebit

Menu Planner
Retro Games Night
(page 19)

An absolute sure crowd-pleaser and ever so comforting. You may need to make two times the amount as your friends will keep coming back for more. Including the Stilton and ale makes these more grown-up. A sprinkle of walnuts for crunch is also a nice touch.

Serves 8

300 g (10½ oz) Stilton, crumbled
300 g (10½ oz) Cheddar, grated
4 tablespoons ale
2 eggs, beaten
2 teaspoons wholegrain mustard
Worcestershire sauce
sea salt and freshly ground black pepper
100 g (3½ oz/⅓ cup) shop-bought red onion marmalade
6–8 slices dark brown thinly sliced bread or rye bread
watercress, to serve (optional)

Heat the grill.

Mix together the cheeses, ale, eggs, mustard and a dash of Worcestershire sauce with some seasoning.

Start by spreading the red onion marmalade onto the slices of bread and cut each slice in half and each half into three – you should be left with 6 squares for each piece of bread. Spread the cheese mixture evenly onto all the bread pieces and put on a baking sheet. Grill for 3–5 minutes until golden brown and bubbling. Serve garnished with watercress, if using.

Serving Tip
Sauté chunky mushrooms, spread them on thickly cut sourdough and top with the rarebit to serve as a main course.

| **V** | | | | **NF** |

Macaroni Cheese Bites

Menu Planner
Lazy Afternoon
(page 19)

These are proper little treats and the ultimate comfort food that can be made in advance and frozen in the mini muffin trays. Take them out and top them with the crumb and bake just before your friends arrive. They are a firm favourite with children too.

Makes 48

50 g (2 oz/scant ¼ cup) butter
50 g (2 oz/scant ½ cup) plain (all-purpose) flour
450 ml (14¾ fl oz/1¾ cups) milk
75 g (2½ oz) gruyère, grated
50 g (2 oz/scant ½ cup) mature Cheddar, grated
1 tablespoon Dijon mustard
¼ teaspoon grated nutmeg
sea salt and freshly ground black pepper
200 g (7 oz/1⅓ cups) macaroni

FOR THE CAYENNE CRUMB
30 g (1 oz/¼ cup) Cheddar, grated
50 g (1 oz/scant 1 cup) panko breadcrumbs
1–2 teaspoons thyme leaves
1 teaspoon chopped rosemary leaves
1 teaspoon cayenne pepper
oil, for greasing

Heat the oven to 180°C (350°F/gas 4).

Melt the butter in a large saucepan, stir in the flour and cook gently for a few minutes, until it forms a ball. Stir in the milk, a little at a time, until it makes a smooth sauce. Cook over a medium heat for 5 minutes, stirring continuously, until thick. Remove from the heat, add the cheeses, mustard, nutmeg and plenty of black pepper. Check the seasoning, adding salt if needed, and set aside.

Meanwhile, cook the macaroni in a large pan of boiling water, following pack instructions. Drain well and add to the cheese sauce; mix to combine. Set aside.

Meanwhile, make the cayenne crumb. Mix the cheddar, breadcrumbs, herbs and cayenne in a small bowl ready to top the macaroni cheese.

Lightly grease two 24-hole mini muffin tins with oil, then fill with the macaroni cheese mixture. Top evenly with the cheesy breadcrumb mixture.

Bake for 18–20 minutes, until golden on top.

Serving Tip
These can be made, topped and frozen for a month in advance if you want to get ahead.

V   **NF**

Ricotta & Caponata

Menu Planner
Elegant Brunch
(page 17)

Sicilian caponata is a dish that can be eaten warm as a side, or cold as an antipasti. It's an ideal partner for baked ricotta and focaccia.

Serves 8

1 whole ricotta
4 tablesooons olive oil
1 lemon, zested and juiced
2 garlic cloves, crushed
25 g (1 oz) basil leaves, shredded
sea salt and freshly ground black
   pepper

FOR THE CAPONATA
2 tablespoons olive oil
2 aubergines (eggplants), cubed
1 red onion, thinly sliced
2 celery stalks, thinly sliced
1 garlic clove, crushed
1 tablespoon tomato purée (paste)
150 g (5 oz/¾ cup) cherry
   tomatoes, halved
1–2 teaspoons honey (or to taste)
100 g (3½ oz) green olives, chopped
40 g (1½ oz) capers, chopped
40 g (1½ oz) raisins, soaked in
   balsamic vinegar for 15 minutes
sea salt and freshly ground black
   pepper

TO SERVE
20 g (¾ oz) pine nuts, toasted
large handful of basil leaves
extra virgin olive oil
1 focaccia loaf, cut into strips

To make the caponata, heat the olive oil in a large frying pan over medium-high heat. Add the aubergine and cook until golden all over, then transfer to a plate with a slotted spoon.

Put the onion, celery and garlic in the frying pan and cook, stirring occasionally, until very tender. Add the tomato purée, cherry tomatoes, honey and 250 ml (8½ fl oz/1 cup) water and simmer until reduced by half. Return the aubergine to the pan and simmer until the mixture is reduced to a thick sauce. Remove from the heat and stir in the olives, capers and raisins with their vinegar. Season to taste and cool to room temperature. Serve scattered with pine nuts and basil, and drizzled with extra-virgin olive oil.

Heat the oven to 180°C (350°F/gas 4).

Line a baking tray with baking parchment. Put the ricotta on the tray and brush with a little of the olive oil. Bake for 30 minutes, or until golden brown. Allow to cool slightly.

Mix the remaining olive oil, lemon juice and zest, crushed garlic and shredded basil in a bowl and season to taste. Place the whole ricotta on a platter and pour on the dressing.

Serve the caponata with the baked ricotta and focaccia strips. Caponata keeps in the refrigerator, covered, for up to 7 days, if you want to get ahead.

Feta & Mint Hummus

Menu Planner
Pre-party
(page 18)

Pimp up your hummus with some extras and a large bowl of crudités. The mint and feta combo gives a fresh twist to everyone's favourite dip.

Makes 4–6

300 g (10½ oz) pot hummus
100 g (3½ oz) feta, crumbled
3 sprigs mint, leaves picked and
    finely chopped
50 g (2 oz/generous ⅓ cup) petits
    pois, defrosted and gently crushed
½ bunch spring onions (scallions),
    thinly sliced

FOR THE TOPPING
1 tablespoon olive oil
50 g (2 oz/generous ⅓ cup) petits
    pois, defrosted
½ bunch spring onions (scallions),
    thinly sliced
handful of mint leaves, chopped,
    to garnish
lemon zest (optional)

In a bowl, mix the hummus, feta, mint, crushed petits pois and spring onions and set aside. In a small frying pan, gently heat the olive oil and add the petits pois and spring onions and cook for a few minutes. Add the mint and zest, top the hummus with it, and serve with the crudités.

| V | | | GF | NF |

Cheesy

Ricotta & Caponata, *page 88*
Chorizo & Goat's Cheese Palmiers, *page 130*

Halloumi Filo Swirls
with Skordalia

Menu Planner
Evening
Soirée
(page 18)

An absolute favourite in our house. The halloumi filo swirls can be shaped
and stored in the freezer and cooked just before serving.

Serves 8

225 g (8 oz/1¾ cups) block
  halloumi, grated
150 g (5 oz/scant ⅔ cup) ricotta
1 egg
2 sprigs mint, leaves picked and
  chopped
8 sheets filo pastry
100 g (3½ oz/generous ⅓ cup)
  unsalted butter, melted
40 g (1½ oz/¼ cup) white sesame
  seeds

FOR THE SKORDALIA
1 slice soft white bread, soaked in
  2 tablespoons milk
1 cooked beetroot, chopped
50 g (2 oz/⅓ cup) toasted almonds,
  coarsely chopped
4 cloves garlic, roasted
200 ml (7 fl oz/scant 1 cup) olive oil
sea salt and freshly ground black
  pepper
1 tablespoon dukkah

Heat the oven to 180°C (350°F/gas 4).

For the filling, mix the halloumi, ricotta, egg and mint in a bowl
and set aside.

Aim to make four swirls using two sheets of filo for each. Start
by laying out a sheet of filo, brushing it with melted butter and
topping it with the second layer of filo. Brush the top of the
second sheet with butter and fold the shortest sides over to
meet in the middle. Spread a quarter of the halloumi filling along
the length, leaving a 3 cm (1¼ in) gap along each edge. Fold in
the sides, then roll up loosely and twist into a coil.

Put on a baking tray lined with baking parchment. Repeat with
the remaining pastry and filling. Brush the tops with butter,
scatter with sesame seeds, and bake until golden.

To make the skordalia, whizz the milk-soaked bread, cooked
beetroot, chopped almonds and roasted garlic in a food
processor until finely chopped, then, with the motor running,
gradually add the oil in a thin, steady stream. Thin it with a little
hot water if necessary. Season to taste. Top with the dukkah.

Serve the swirls straight from the oven with the skordalia on
the side.

V   **NF**

Quail's Eggs
with Avocado & Yuzu Whip

Quail's eggs are fun but fiddly to peel. I buy them cooked and peeled and serve them simply, with the yuzu and avocado whip. You could also cook small hen's eggs and halve them as an alternative.

Menu Planner
Casual Christmas Drinks
(page 17)

Serves 8

2 × packets of 12 quail's eggs (ready cooked and peeled)

FOR THE AVOCADO & YUZU WHIP
2 avocados, pitted and peeled
1 lime, juiced
2 tablespoons tahini
1–2 teaspoons yuzu juice (or to taste), plus extra to finish

TO SERVE
sesame oil
1 tablespoon mixed black and white sesame seeds

Combine all of the avocado & yuzu whip ingredients a food processor and whizz until smooth (about 30 seconds). Transfer to serving dish. (To make up to 6 hours ahead, set aside 1 tablespoon lime juice; drizzle it over the surface and cover with cling film (plastic wrap). Refrigerate.)

Serve the whip topped with sesame oil and an extra drizzle of yuzu alongside the quail's eggs and sprinkle with the sesame seeds.

| V | | GF | | NF |

Wild Mushroom Tartlets

Menu Planner
Casual
Christmas
Drinks
(page 17)

You can't go wrong with the classic flavours of mushrooms, goat's cheese and figs. Shop-bought cases really speed things up, but you can use layers of butter-brushed filo pastry in mini-muffin tins, if you like.

Makes 24

24 mini croustade cups or other
   shop-bought pastry shells

FOR THE MUSHROOM FILLING
2 tablespoons olive oil
1 onion, finely chopped
sea salt and freshly ground black
   pepper
250 g (9 oz/3 cups) mixed wild
   mushrooms
1 garlic clove, crushed
3–4 tablespoons thyme leaves
   (reserving some, to serve)
4 figs, sliced into 12 rounds
150 g (5¼ oz) log goat's cheese,
   sliced into 24 small pieces

TO SERVE
honey, to drizzle

For the filling, heat the oil in a frying pan, add the onion and fry over a moderate heat until soft and golden, and add seasoning to taste. Turn up the heat and add the mushrooms. Sizzle for a few minutes until any moisture has cooked off and the mushrooms are golden. Stir in the garlic, cook for a few minutes, then turn off the heat and stir in most of the thyme leaves.

Divide the mushroom mixture between the tart cases and top with the goat's cheese and the fig rounds. Bake for 10–15 minutes until golden and bubbling. Sprinkle over remaining thyme leaves, drizzle with honey and serve.

V   **NF**

Vegetarian

Wild Mushrooms Tartlets, *page 95*

98

Root Vegetable & Sage Fritters

Menu Planner
Casual Christmas Drinks
(*page 17*)
&
Elegant Brunch
(*page 17*)

This fritter recipe is very adaptable to whatever root vegetables you have. I like the combination of carrot, sweet potato and parsnip with cranberry and blue cheese topping. The fritters can be cooked and cooled and put in the refrigerator on a tray to be reheated when your guests arrive up to 24 hours in advance.

Serves 8

3 tablespoons olive oil
1 onion, thinly sliced
1 garlic clove, crushed
500 g (1 lb 2 oz/4 cups) grated root
   vegetables, e.g. 1–2 carrots,
   1 sweet potato and 1 parsnip
70 g (2¼ oz) Parmesan (or vegan
   or vegetarian alternative), coarsely
   grated
1 lemon, zested
100 g (3½ oz/generous ¾ cup) plain
   (all-purpose) flour
2 tablespoons chopped sage leaves
1 tablespoon thyme leaves
sea salt and freshly ground black
   pepper

FOR THE TOPPING
100 g (3½ oz) cranberry sauce
100 g (3½ oz) blue cheese (or a
   vegetarian or vegan alternative),
   crumbled
8 sage leaves

Heat 1 tablespoon olive oil in a pan over medium-high heat, add the onion and garlic and sauté until tender. Tip into a large bowl, add the carrot, sweet potato, parsnip, Parmesan, lemon zest, flour, chopped sage and thyme leaves, season and mix well. Form into walnut-sized patties and set aside on a tray.

Heat the rest of the olive oil in a clean frying pan over medium-high heat, add the sage leaves and fry until crisp. Drain on paper towels.

Add the patties to the pan in batches and fry until golden brown on both sides and cooked through. Drain on paper towels, season to taste.

Top each fritter with a spoon of cranberry sauce, crumbled blue cheese and crushed crispy sage leaves.

| V | | | | NF |

Vegetarian

Potsticker Dumplings

These can be simply steamed instead but the steam-frying method gives a delicious crispness to the base of these potstickers – and you only need one pan to cook them.

Makes 30

5 tablespoons vegetable oil
250 g (9 oz/3 cups) mushrooms, finely chopped
100 g (3½ oz/1⅓ cups) Asian cabbage, shredded
2 garlic cloves, crushed
2 spring onions (scallions), finely chopped
1 thumb-sized piece fresh ginger root, peeled and grated
1 tablespoon kecap manis
90 g (3¼ oz/½ cup) water chestnuts, finely chopped
30 shop-bought gow gee or gyoza wrappers
250 ml (8½ fl oz/1 cup) water

TO SERVE
steamed greens
chilli soy sauce
toasted sesame seeds

Heat 2 tablespoons vegetable oil in a large saucepan then gently fry the mushrooms for a few minutes. Add the shredded cabbage, garlic, spring onions, ginger, kecap manis and water chestnuts and allow to soften. They need not be fully cooked just all melded nicely. Allow to cool.

Place the gow gee wrappers on a clean work surface and brush the edges of each wrapper with water. Place 2 teaspoons of the vegetable mixture in the centre of each wrapper and pinch the sides together to seal. Set aside.

Heat 1½ tablespoons oil in a 16 cm (6½ in) non-stick frying pan over medium heat. Add half the dumplings, flat-side down, and cook for 3 minutes. Pour over half the water, cover with a tight-fitting lid and cook for a further 3 minutes. Uncover and cook for 3–4 minutes more or until the water has evaporated and dumplings are golden and crispy on the bottom.

Put the cooked dumplings on a plate and repeat with the remaining oil and water.

Serve on a plate with steamed greens, chilli soy sauce and toasted sesame seeds.

V | **VG** | **DF**

Crispy Tofu
with Watercress Dipping Sauce

Menu Planner
Evening Soirée
(page 18)

For a vegan version of this dish omit bread-crumbing the tofu as egg-whites are used for this. Fried tofu is still as delicious served with the cucumber salad and watercress dipping sauce.

Serves 8

50 g (2 oz/²⁄₃ cup) breadcrumbs
sea salt and freshly ground black pepper
2 egg whites
600 g (1 lb 5 oz/2²⁄₃ cups) firm tofu, drained and cubed
2 tablespoons vegetable oil
1 teaspoon sesame oil
2 tablespoons mirin
1 thumb-sized piece ginger root, peeled and grated
200 g (7 oz) cucumber, thinly sliced
1 bunch mint, leaves picked

FOR THE DIPPING SAUCE
1 handful watercress, finely chopped
2 tablespoons light soy sauce
1 small red chilli, finely chopped
1 tablespoon sesame oil

To make the dipping sauce, put the watercress, soy sauce, chilli and sesame oil in a small bowl. Mix to combine and set aside.

Put the breadcrumbs, salt and pepper in a bowl and mix to combine.

Put the egg whites in a bowl and whisk until fluffy. Dip the tofu cubes in the egg white and press into the breadcrumb mixture.

Heat the vegetable oil in a large non-stick frying pan over high heat. Fry the tofu, in batches, for 1–2 minutes on each side or until golden and crisp. Drain on paper towels and keep warm.

Put the sesame oil, mirin and ginger in a medium bowl and whisk together. Add the cucumber and mint and toss to combine.

Serve the tofu with the cucumber salad and the watercress dipping sauce.

V | | | **DF** | **NF**

Vegetarian

Sausage Rolls
with Harissa Salsa

Gluten-free and vegetarian but full of fun and festiveness. If you have meat-lovers coming, wrap a piece thinly sliced pancetta round each individual sausage roll and tuck in a sage leaf.

Menu Planner
Casual
Christmas Drinks
(page 17)

Makes 18

250 g (9 oz/generous 2⅔ cups) mushrooms
1 aubergine (eggplant), chopped
2 tablespoons olive oil
1 leek, thinly sliced
sea salt
2 garlic cloves
1 tablespoon chopped sage
1 tablespoon brown rice miso
50 g (2 oz/⅓ cup) cooked chestnuts, finely chopped
freshly ground black pepper
70 g (2¼ oz/scant ¾ cup) gluten-free breadcrumbs
2 sheets gluten-free puff pastry
gluten-free flour, to dust
3 tablespoons dairy-free milk, to glaze

FOR THE HARISSA SALSA
200 g (7 oz) jar shop-bought salsa
1–2 tablespoons harissa paste
30 g (1½ oz) mixed fresh herbs, such as mint, coriander and parsley

Tip the mushrooms and aubergine into a food processor and pulse until very finely chopped. Heat the olive oil in a large frying pan, add the leek, along with a pinch of salt, and fry gently for 15 minutes or until softened and golden brown. Add the garlic, sage, miso and chopped chestnuts and fry for a further minute. Leave to cool slightly. Season, then mix everything together until you have a slightly stiff mixture.

Heat the oven to 180°C (350°F/gas 4).

Unravel the pastry on a floured surface, then roll the pastry out so that one side measures 43 cm (17 in). Mould the mushroom and leek mixture into a sausage shape down the centre of the pastry, then bring the pastry up around the filling and seal along the seam with a fork. Cut into 18 pieces on the diagonal. Lay on a baking parchment-lined baking sheet and brush each piece with dairy-free milk. Bake for 25 minutes or until deep golden brown.

For the harissa salsa, mix the salsa with the harissa paste and fresh herbs.

Put the sausage rolls on a board or platter and serve with the harissa salsa in a serving bowl.

V | VG | DF | GF

Rainbow Fresh Spring Rolls
with Spicy Peach Dressing

Vibrant, fresh, colourful and super-tasty, these spring rolls work perfectly with a spicy peach dressing, but if you're pushed for time, sweet chilli sauce works too.

Menu Planner
Elegant
Brunch
(page 17)

Makes 12

12 rice paper spring roll wrappers
1 bunch mint
1 bunch Thai basil
4 spring onions (scallions),
    cut diagonally
1 yellow courgette (zucchini),
    shredded
1 large carrot, peeled and shredded
½ mango, cut into strips
1 red chilli, de-seeded, cut into strips
30 g (1 oz) roasted cashews,
    chopped
edible flowers (optional)

FOR THE SPICY PEACH DRESSING
5 peaches, halved and pitted
1 red onion, cut into wedges
2 cloves garlic, crushed
2 tablespoons mixed spice
1 teaspoon chilli flakes
50 g (2 oz/¼ cup) dark brown sugar
80 ml (2¾ fl oz/5½ tablespoons)
    cider vinegar
sea salt and freshly ground black
    pepper

Have all your ingredients prepared and ready to go before you start assembling the rolls. Dip a spring roll wrapper into a shallow bowl of water until it just softens (don't leave it too long or you'll be left with a gluey mess). Put the wet wrapper on a chopping board, then top with a couple of mint and basil leaves, the spring onions and some courgette, carrot, mango, chilli and roasted cashews and edible flowers, if using.

Starting with the edge nearest to you, fold the wrapper into the centre so that it covers half the filling. Fold in both of the shorter ends, then, rolling away from you, fold the wrapper over so that the entire filling is encased. Repeat with the remaining wrappers and fillings to make 12 spring rolls. These can be made in the morning and kept in the refrigerator for later.

For the spicy peach dressing, put all of the ingredients in a baking dish and bake for 20–30 minutes at 180°C (350°F/gas 4). Allow to cool a little, then blitz into a sauce in a food processor. At this point, taste the sauce and check the balance of sweet and sour and adjust by adding a little more vinegar or sugar and some seasoning.

Cut the spring rolls in half on the diagonal. Serve with spicy peach dipping sauce on the side.

| **V** | **VG** | **DF** | **GF** |

Sweet Potato Pies
with Fresh Mango Salsa

Menu
Planner
Lazy
Afternoon
(page 19)

This is the perfect make-ahead and freeze recipe. In fact the flavours infuse nicer. Baked and then served with a super fresh mango salsa – these will be an absolute crowd pleaser. A lovely alternative to the salsa is a good–quality mango chutney.

Makes 12

1 × 250 g (9 oz) pack ready-rolled, gluten-free pastry

FOR THE FILLING
1 tablespoon olive oil
1 onion, finely chopped
2 sweet potatoes, peeled and finely chopped
2 tablespoons mild curry powder
1 teaspoon garam masala
2 garlic cloves, crushed
200 g (7 oz/1 cup) cherry tomatoes, halved
400 ml (14 fl oz) tin coconut milk
100 g (3½ oz/2⅔ cup) petits pois
20 g (¾ oz/⅔ cup) coriander (cilantro) leaves, chopped
sea salt

FOR THE FRESH MANGO SALSA
1 large mango, peeled and diced
1 red onion, finely chopped
2 limes, juiced
1 red chilli, de-seeded, chopped
8 cherry tomatoes, quartered
1 bunch coriander (cilantro) leaves, picked and chopped
2 tablespoons olive oil
sea salt

To make the filling, heat the oil in a large pan over a low heat and add the onion. Fry gently for until softened. Add the sweet potato, curry powder, garam masala and garlic and continue to fry for 5 minutes, stirring often. Add the cherry tomatoes and coconut milk, bring to a simmer and cook, covered, for about 20 minutes until the sweet potatoes are tender, then add the petits pois. Once cooked, allow to cool then refrigerate until completely cold, then add the coriander.

Roll out the pastry and, using a 7 cm (2¾ in) round cutter, cut out 12 rounds. Put a spoonful of the cooled filling mixture just off-centre of each round of pastry. Brush a little water around the rim of each pasty and fold it over the filling. Press the edges together to seal. Put the pies on a couple of baking sheets lined with baking parchment and refrigerate for half an hour.

Meanwhile, heat the oven to 180°C (350°F/gas 4).

Brush the tops of the pasties with a little dairy-free milk, then bake for 30–40 minutes until golden brown. Set aside to cool for about 10 minutes before serving.

For the fresh mango salsa, mix all the ingredients together and serve alongside the curried sweet potato parcels.

V | VG | DF | GF | NF

105

Rainbow Fresh Spring Rolls with Spicy Peach Dressing, *page 104*
Sweet Potato Pies with Fresh Mango Salsa, *page 105*

Broccoli Spears
with Walnut Babaganoush

Once you make this you won't be able to stop! Serve on a board with the walnut babaganoush, Arabic-style crunchy vegetable pickles and seeded crackers.

Serves 8

2 large heads of broccoli, cut into
   large florets
1 tablespoon ground cumin
1 tablespoon ground coriander
2 teaspoons ground cardamom
1 teaspoon sumac
½ teaspoon ground cinnamon
½ teaspoon nutmeg, grated
sea salt and freshly ground black
   pepper
3 tablespoons olive oil

FOR THE WALNUT BABAGANOUSH
2 aubergines (eggplants)
100 g (3½ oz/1 cup) walnuts,
   soaked in cold water for
   10 minutes
2 tablespoons tahini
1 clove garlic, crushed
2 teaspoons ground cumin
1 teaspoon ground coriander
½ teaspoon sumac
1 lemon, juiced
1–2 tablespoons olive oil

TO SERVE
100 g (3½ oz) Arabic-style pickled
   vegetables
6–8 seeded crackers

Heat the oven to 200°C (400°F/gas 6).

Toss the broccoli, spices and oil on a baking sheet; season with salt and pepper. Roast, tossing occasionally, until tender and browned, 15–20 minutes.

For the walnut babaganoush, make a slit in the aubergines and cook in a very hot oven for 35–40 minutes or char on a hot griddle pan. Peel off the charred skin and chop the flesh. Tip into a food processor with the walnuts, tahini, garlic, cumin, ground coriander, sumac and lemon juice and season to taste.

Spoon the walnut babaganoush dip onto a large platter, drizzle with olive oil and serve with the broccoli, crackers and pickles.

| **V** | **VG** | **DF** | **GF** |

Vegan Mushroom & Port Pâté

with Crunchy Crackers

Whether you are vegan or not, this pâté is delicious! The crackers are so satisfying to make yourself, but you can always buy some and just make the pâté.

Serves 8

120 g (4¼ oz/generous ¾ cup) wholemeal flour

50 g (2 oz/scant ½ cup) ground almonds

¼ teaspoon baking powder

20 g (¾ oz/scant ¼ cup) ground flaxseeds

1 teaspoon picked rosemary leaves

a few pinches of sea salt

3 tablespoons olive oil

FOR THE MUSHROOM AND PORT PATE

1 tablespoon vegan margarine

1 onion, thinly sliced

400 g (14 oz) chestnut (cremini) mushrooms, thinly sliced

3 garlic cloves, crushed

3 tablespoons port

2 sprigs rosemary, leaves picked

1½ tablespoons breadcrumbs

2 tablespoons lemon juice

sea salt and freshly ground black pepper

TO SERVE

handful of mixed herbs

Heat the oven to 160°C (320°F/gas 3).

Blitz the all the dry cracker ingredients in a food processor until well combined. Then add oil and pulse, adding 3½ tablespoons cold water, one spoon at a time. Pulsing will form a semi-sticky dough that's mouldable with your hands and not crumbly. Take it out of the processor and transfer it to a clean work surface lined with baking parchment. Lay another sheet of baking parchment on top and use a rolling pin to roll the dough out into a rectangle. Using a knife, cut it into rectangles. Transfer the rolled-out dough to a baking sheet and put it in the freezer for about 10 minutes to firm up. Take off the top sheet of baking parchment and bake for 16–22 minutes, or until slightly golden brown, then take it out of the oven and leave to cool. Store in an airtight container for up to a week.

For the mushroom and port pâté, heat the margarine in a large frying pan, add the onion and cook until softened, then turn up the heat and add the mushrooms. Once the mushrooms have released their juices, add the garlic and port and cook down until it has reduced, then add the rosemary, breadcrumbs and lemon juice and allow to cool a little. Blitz in a food processor to the consistency you like – I prefer it to be smooth – and season. Put it in a sterilised jar and keep in the fridge for up to 3 days.

Plate the crackers topped with mushroom pâté, a drizzle with olive oil and a scattering of fresh herbs, if you like.

| **V** | **VG** | **DF** | | |

Polenta Squares
with Roasted Cherry Tomatoes

This is gluten-free, comforting and elegant at the same time. The flavours are timeless. For an extra kick, add a few pinches of chilli flakes and honey when roasting the cherry tomatoes.

Serves 8

400 ml (13 fl oz/generous 1½ cups) milk
400 ml (13 fl oz/generous 1½ cups) vegetable stock
3 sprigs rosemary, leaves picked and chopped
4 sprigs thyme, leaves picked
150 g (5 oz/1 cup) polenta
40 g (1½ oz) butter
60 g (2 oz) Parmesan, grated
pinch of nutmeg, freshly grated
olive oil, for greasing
sea salt and freshly ground black pepper

FOR THE ROASTED CHERRY TOMATOES
200 g (7 oz) cherry tomatoes on the vine
1 tablespoon olive oil
sea salt and freshly ground black pepper
50 g (2 oz) Parmesan, shaved
1 bunch basil, leaves picked

Put the milk, stock and chopped rosemary in a pan and heat to just boiling point. Sprinkle the polenta into the pan in a slow, steady stream, stirring continuously for 3–5 minutes – the polenta will swell and thicken. Keep stirring for 10–15 minutes over a low heat. Once the grains are less visible and the polenta starts to become smooth, reduce the heat to very low and cook for 10 minutes more, beating it frequently. Add some extra water to loosen the mixture if necessary.

Meanwhile, line a 20 × 25 cm (8 × 10 in) baking tray with baking parchment and grease the parchment with the olive oil. When the polenta is cooked, smooth and slick, add the butter and the Parmesan and beat well, season with nutmeg and salt, then pour it into the lined tray. Use a palette knife or the back of a spoon to push and smooth the polenta into the corners to an even depth of about 2.5 cm (1 in). Leave to cool, then put in the refrigerator to set for at least 30 minutes, or overnight.

Heat the oven to 180°C (350°F/gas 6).

Put the cherry tomatoes on a baking tray, drizzle with olive oil, season, and roast for 10 minutes.

Meanwhile, turn out the polenta onto a chopping board and cut into 5 cm (2 in) squares. Put them, smooth-side up, on a larger, lightly oiled baking sheet and bake in the oven until crisp (about 15 minutes).

Serve topped with the roasted cherry tomatoes, shaved Parmesan and basil.

V   **GF**   **NF**

Five Spice Duck Pancakes
with Plum Sauce

Menu Planner
Retro Games Night
(page 19)

Healthier than a takeaway (take out) and an easy dish to share. Using just breasts of duck makes it a much quicker dish to prepare. You could use shop-bought plum or hoisin sauce instead of making it from scratch.

Serves 8

3 tablespoons maple syrup
2 tablespoons honey
2 tablespoons five spice powder
2 garlic cloves, crushed to a paste
3 duck breasts, skin-on

FOR THE PLUM SAUCE
5 plums, halved and stoned
1 tablespoon maple syrup
1 tablespoon honey
2 tablespoons soy sauce
1 teaspoon ground ginger
1 teaspoon five-spice powder
½ teaspoon ground cinnamon
pinch of chilli flakes

TO SERVE
1 large cucumber, cut into
  matchsticks
1 bunch spring onions (scallions),
  cleaned and cut into matchsticks
1 green chilli, cut into strips
  (optional)
30 shop-bought Chinese-style
  pancakes
1 bunch chives

Heat the oven to 180°C (350°F/gas 4).

Mix the maple syrup, honey, five spice powder and garlic paste in a bowl, then brush all over the duck breasts. Transfer to a roasting tin and roast for 25–30 minutes until bronzed. Allow to cool, then shred.

While the duck is cooking, put all the plum sauce ingredients in a saucepan and simmer gently for 15 minutes or until the plums are soft and the sauce is thick. Allow to cool a little and blitz in a blender until thick.

Spread each pancake with a little plum sauce. Top with the shredded duck, a few pieces of cucumber, spring onion and chilli if using, and, for a fun touch, tie with a chive.

| | | DF | | NF |

Chicken, Artichoke & Olive Pâté

This is a lighter pâté using chicken breast, artichokes, olives and basil. It's fresh and a nice alternative to chicken liver pâté. It can be made a day in advance.

Serves 8

1 baguette or ciabatta, thinly sliced
4 tablespoons extra virgin olive oil
1 garlic clove, cut in half lengthways
sea salt and freshly ground black
   pepper

FOR THE PATE
300 g (10½ oz) skinless, boneless
   chicken breast
500 ml (17 fl oz/2 cups) vegetable
   stock
1 small carrot, peeled
1 stalk celery, cut in half, widthways
3 tablespoons butter
1 banana shallot, finely chopped
100 g (3½ oz/scant half cup)
   artichoke hearts, from a tin or jar,
   drained
1 tablespoon olive oil
½ teaspoon grated nutmeg
pinch ground mace
50 g (2 oz/scant ¼ cup) green
   olives, pitted and sliced
½ bunch basil, chopped

TO SERVE
Micro herbs

To make the crostini, brush the slices of the baguette or ciabatta on each side with olive oil, then grill on each side until golden. Rub lightly with the cut surfaces of the garlic clove and brush with the rest of the extra virgin olive oil.

In a saucepan, poach the chicken breast in the stock with the carrot and celery for 25–30 minutes, until fully cooked. Turn off the heat and allow to cool down in the stock.

Meanwhile, gently fry the shallots in butter for 6–7 minutes, or until softened, and allow to cool.

Once the chicken has cooled, take it out of the stock (reserving the stock), roughly chop the chicken, and put it in the bowl of a food processor. Add the cooked shallots and butter, artichokes, olive oil, nutmeg and mace, and pulse to a coarse consistency. If you would like to loosen the mixture, add some of the reserved stock. Add the chopped olives and basil and pulse one or two more times. Transfer to a jar or bowl and put in the refrigerator. Don't throw the stock away – freeze it in ice-cube trays to use in the future to add to stews or soups.

Serve the crostini topped with pâté, pepper and micro-herbs.

NF

Thai Meatballs
with Coriander Dressing

Traditionally made with pork, this turkey mince version is lighter and less fatty. Serve with the coriander dressing to dip them into.

Makes 24

1 green chilli, seeded and diced
3 lemongrass stalks, chopped
1 thumb-sized piece fresh ginger
   root, peeled and grated
½ bunch coriander (cilantro)
500 g (1 lb 2 oz) turkey mince
sea salt and freshly ground black
   pepper
1 tablespoon each sesame oil, fish
   sauce, soy sauce
1 teaspoon palm or brown sugar
50 g (2 oz/generous ¾ cup) panko
   breadcrumbs, soaked in water
1 egg, lightly whisked
2 tablespoons vegetable oil

FOR THE CORIANDER DRESSING
1 tablespoon palm sugar
3 tablespoons fish sauce
2 tablespoons rice wine vinegar
5½ tablespoons water
1 bird's eye chilli
½ bunch coriander (cilantro), leaves
   picked and finely chopped

TO SERVE
1 lettuce, leaves separated
grated carrot and sliced cucumber
handful of bean sprouts (optional)

Put the chilli, lemongrass, ginger and half bunch of coriander in a small blender. Blitz until smooth, then transfer to a bowl with the turkey mince. Season well and add the sesame oil, fish sauce, soy sauce, soaked breadcrumbs and the egg and mix well. Roll into 24 small meatballs. Heat some oil and cook for 5–6 minutes on each side and completely cooked-through.

For the coriander dressing, mix all the ingredients in a bowl, reserving the chopped coriander to stir in just before you serve the sauce.

Serve the meatballs on a bed of lettuce leaves and grated carrot and finish with bean sprouts if you like. Serve alongside the coriander dipping sauce.

DF   **NF**

Date & Pomegranate Chicken Wings

Menu Planner
Lazy Afternoon
(page 19)

Super-sticky and mouth-watering, these wings are not for people who don't like getting their hands dirty when they eat! They are so worth it.

Serves 8

4 tablespoons pomegranate molasses
4 tablespoons date syrup
2 garlic cloves, crushed to a paste
2 tablespoons olive oil
½ teaspoon ground cinnamon
1 teaspoon chilli flakes
½ teaspoon freshly ground black pepper
sea salt
1 kg (2 lb 4 oz) chicken wings

TO SERVE
½ bunch spring onions (scallions), finely sliced
80 g (3 oz/½ cup) pomegranate seeds
30 g (1 oz/scant ¼ cup) pistachios, roughly chopped
handful mixed mint and coriander (cilantro) leaves

Mix the pomegranate molasses, date syrup, garlic paste, olive oil, cinnamon, chilli flakes, black pepper and pinch of salt together in a large mixing bowl. Add the chicken wings and mix well so that everything gets completely coated in the marinade. Cover and chill in the refrigerator for 30 minutes, or overnight.

Heat the oven to 200°C (400°F/gas 6).

Take the chicken out of the refrigerator and allow it to come to room temperature while the oven heats. Tip it into a roasting tin and roast in the oven for 20 minutes, or until it's cooked through and tender, with no pink meat.

Transfer the wings to a serving dish and spoon over the sticky juices from the tin. Scatter over the sliced spring onions, pomegranate seeds, pistachios and mint and coriander leaves. Serve immediately.

DF | **GF**

Korean Ssam Chicken Skewers

with Kimchi Miso Dressing

This is a hybrid Asian barbecue-flavoured recipe. The kimchi miso dressing finishes it nicely. If you're pushed for time, serve each skewer with a piece or two of kimchi for extra punch.

Serves 8

50 g (2 oz/scant ¼ cup) gluten-free gochujang

50 g (2 oz/scant ¼ cup) gluten-free barbecue sauce (good quality shop-bought)

2 tablespoons mirin

1 lime, juiced

1½ tablespoons sesame oil

1 thumb-sized piece fresh ginger root, peeled and grated

1 kg (2 lb 4 oz) chicken thigh fillets, cut into bite-sized pieces

100 g (3½ oz) mini courgettes (zucchini)

FOR THE KIMCHI MISO DRESSING

4 tablespoons white miso

1 tablespoon vegetable oil

1 tablespoon tahini

1 tablespoon rice vinegar

sea salt

70–100 g (2½–3½ oz) kimchi, depending on taste

For the chicken ssam, combine all of the ingredients except the chicken and courgettes in a large bowl, then add the chicken and mix well to coat. Transfer to an airtight container and refrigerate for at least an hour, but preferably overnight, to marinate.

For the kimchi dressing, whisk all the ingredients except the kimchi in a bowl to combine. Put the kimchi and the whisked mixture in a blender and purée until very smooth – at this stage you may have to add water to loosen it; season with salt. Refrigerate until ready to use. The dressing may thicken as it sits – before serving, thin it with water if you need to.

Soak some wooden skewers in water for 30 minutes, then thread a piece or 2 of chicken and a piece of courgette onto the skewers. Drizzle with oil and cook in a griddle pan or on the barbecue, turning occasionally, until charred and cooked through.

Serve the skewers hot, with the kimchi dressing.

DF | **GF** | **NF**

COCKTAILS & CANAPES

Mini Schnitzels

Classic but not outdated – you can never tire of schnitzel and remoulade. If there are any leftovers, they're perfect on a sandwich with buttered white bread. It's also gluten-free.

Menu Planner
Elegant
Brunch
(page 17)

Serves 8

FOR THE REMOULADE
1 small celeriac, julienned
1 green apple, julienned
1 lemon, zested and juiced
sea salt
60 g (2 oz/¼ cup) each mayonnaise
    and crème fraîche
1 teaspoon sugar
1 tablespoon Dijon mustard
2–3 small gherkins (cornichons),
    finely chopped
freshly ground black pepper
1 handful flat–leaf parsley leaves,
    chopped

FOR THE SCHNITZEL
500 g (1 lb 2 oz) mini chicken breast
    fillets
sea salt and freshly ground black
    pepper
100 g (3½ oz) gluten-free plain
    (all purpose) flour
1 egg, whisked
200 g (7 oz/2 cups) gluten-free
    breadcrumbs
25 g (1 oz) Parmesan, grated
1 teaspoon dried oregano
handful parsley leaves, finely
    chopped
vegetable oil, for frying

To make the remoulade, mix the celeriac and apple with the lemon juice and a generous pinch of salt. Mix in the mayonnaise, crème fraîche, sugar, mustard, gherkins and a turn of black pepper. Taste and adjust the seasoning if needed and set aside, reserving the herbs to finish before serving. This makes extra but keeps in the refrigerator for up to a week (it's perfect on sandwiches, served alongside ham or boiled eggs).

For the schnitzels, season the chicken breasts well with salt and pepper. Tip the flour into a shallow bowl, the egg into another, and tip the breadcrumbs, Parmesan, oregano and parsley into a third and mix well.

Turn the breasts, one at a time, in the flour until evenly coated, shaking away the excess. Dip and drag each one through the egg so that it is coated, drip away the excess and put into the breadcrumbs, turning and pressing until completely coated.

Heat the oil in a large frying pan over a medium–high heat and cook the chicken schnitzels, a few at a time, for 2–3 minutes on each side until completely golden, then lift out onto paper towels to drain. You can keep them warm in a low oven while you cook the rest.

To serve, put the mini chicken schnitzels on a platter with the remoulade, garnished with parsley.

GF | **NF**

Prawn Cocktail Cups

Menu Planner
Casual Christmas Drinks
(page 17)

Transport yourself to the 1960s with this retro classic. Griddling the prawns adds a depth of flavour, but this is just as delicious if you use shop-bought, ready-cooked prawns, in which case you will only need half the amount of olive oil.

Makes 24

24 raw king tiger prawns, peeled
3 tablespoons olive oil
2 tablespoons lemon juice
sea salt and freshly ground black pepper
4 tablespoons chopped parsley

FOR THE MARIE ROSE SAUCE
100 g (3½ oz/generous ⅓ cup) mayonnaise
2 tablespoons ketchup
2 dashes Tabasco sauce

TO SERVE
4–6 little gems (bibb lettuces), leaves separated
handful of cress
fresh horseradish, grated, to taste

To make the marie rose sauce, mix the mayonnaise with the ketchup and a couple of shakes of Tabasco sauce in a bowl.

Toss the uncooked prawns in another bowl with half the olive oil and season, heat a griddle pan and griddle the prawns on each side until fully cooked. Toss the prawns in a bowl with the remaining olive oil, lemon juice, parsley and a little more seasoning.

Lay the lettuce leaves out on serving plates, cupped-side up. Drop several prawns into each. Dollop half a teaspoon of marie rose sauce on top. These can be prepared an hour in advance, in which case, cover with cling film (plastic wrap) and set aside in a cool place. When ready to serve, finish with a scattering of cress and grated horseradish.

DF | GF | NF

Smoked Trout Blinis

with Pickled Cucumber

Menu Planner
Casual
Christmas
Drinks
(page 17)

For a traditional Russian blini recipe, I use Delia Smith's as I have tried so many and this is by far my favourite. They are fun to make, and the addition of buckwheat is what really makes them. No judgement if you buy them – ultimately it's about spending time with your friends.

Makes 18–20

200 g (7 oz) smoked trout
100 g (3½ oz/generous ⅓ cup)
  crème fraîche
1 shallot, finely chopped
1 lemon, zested and juiced
½ bunch dill, finely chopped
sea salt and freshly ground black
  pepper

FOR THE PICKLED CUCUMBER
3 tablespoons apple cider vinegar
2 teaspoons sugar
3 Lebanese mini-cucumbers, thinly
  sliced

TO SERVE
20 blinis made to Delia Smith's
  recipe, or shop-bought
caviar (optional)

Dice the trout and set aside. Mix the crème fraîche in a bowl with the shallot, lemon juice, dill and salt and pepper and set aside.

Mix the vinegar and sugar in a bowl, add the cucumber, and allow to sit for half an hour before serving.

Gently heat the blinis according to pack instructions, and allow to cool a little.

To assemble, place the blinis on plates, add some diced trout, top with a little spoonful of the crème fraîche and finish with pickled cucumber and caviar, if using.

 NF

123

Prawn Cocktail Cups, *page 122*
Smoked Trout Blinis with Pickled Cucumber, *page 122*

Keralan-style Prawns

Menu
Planner
Evening
Soirée
(page 18)

There are Keralan vibes with these green peppercorn and curry leaf prawns. They are perfect on the barbecue or griddled for some charred flavour and then dipped in to some mango chutney.

Makes 20

20 raw prawns, peeled, tail on

1 bunch of spring onions (scallions), each cut into 3 pieces

1 lime, juiced

2 garlic cloves, crushed

1 thumb-sized piece fresh ginger root, peeled and grated

½ teaspoon ground turmeric

2 tablespoons green peppercorns in brine, drained and rinsed

1 teaspoon sea salt

8 fried curry leaves (or a sprig of fresh ones), plus extra, to serve

20 small bamboo skewers, soaked in water for 30 minutes

TO SERVE

4 limes, cut into wedges

30 g (1½ oz) coriander (cilantro)

In a bowl combine the prawns, spring onions, lime juice, garlic, ginger and turmeric. Put in the refrigerator for 25 minutes.

Lightly crush the green peppercorns and salt to a paste then mix well with the prawns and the curry leaves. Thread 1 prawn on each bamboo skewer followed by 3 pieces of spring onion. Heat a barbecue, griddle pan or oven grill to very hot and cook the prawns for 30 seconds each side until just done.

Serve with extra lime and coriander and curry leaves.

Serving Tip

These look great served in copper mugs or tins with extra curry leaves, coriander leaves and lime wedges.

DF | **GF** | **NF**

Gin & Honey Gravadlax

Menu
Planner
Retro
Games
Night
(page 19)

Gravadlax is always a show-stopper and a great way to feed a crowd. This elegant canapé sees it served with whipped cream cheese and soft herbs such as flat-leaf parsley, tarragon, chervil, dill and chives.

Serves 10

2 tablespoons gin
2 tablespoons wholegrain mustard
2 tablespoons honey
100 g (3½ oz/¾ cup) sea salt flakes
100 g (3¾ oz/scant ⅓ cup) caster (superfine) sugar
1 bunch dill, chopped
1 teaspoon juniper berries, crushed
1.1 kg (2 lb 7½ oz) salmon fillet, skin on

FOR THE GIN AND HONEY GLAZE
2 tablespoons gin
2 tablespoons honey
3 tablespoons finely chopped dill

FOR THE WHIPPED CREAM CHEESE
150 g (5 oz/⅔ cup) cream cheese
100 ml (3½ fl oz/⅓ cup) sour cream
1 teaspoon pink peppercorns, crushed
1 lemon, zested and juiced

FOR THE SOFT HERB SALAD
100 g (3½ oz) mixed soft herbs
reserved lemon juice (as above)
2–3 tablespoons olive oil

For the gravadlax, combine the gin, mustard and honey in a small bowl. In another bowl combine the salt, sugar, dill and crushed juniper berries. Lay the salmon fillet flat in a large dish, skin-side down. Spread the gin, mustard and honey mixture over the fillet and sprinkle with the salt mixture. Put the fish in a shallow baking dish or shallow-sided tray and cover tightly in cling film (plastic wrap). Lay another tray on top. Weigh the tray down with a couple of tins and put in the refrigerator for at least 48 hours or up to three days, turning the fish over every 12 hours.

When you are ready to serve, make the gin and honey glaze. In a bowl, combine the gin and honey.

Rinse the salmon fillet thoroughly under cold running water. Pat dry with paper towels. Return to the cleaned dish and brush with the gin and honey glaze. Sprinkle with the dill.

For the whipped cream cheese, whisk the cream cheese, sour cream, crushed pink peppercorns and lemon zest in a mixer using the whisk attachment, and put in a bowl.

Just before serving, put the herbs in a bowl and drizzle with the lemon juice and olive oil. Thinly slice the gravadlax and serve with the cream cheese and soft herb salad.

Serving Tip
Have a few rye crackers on hand for people to pile the salmon and whipped cream cheese onto, or have mini forks next to it.

NF

Smoked Mackerel Pâté
on Melba Toasts

These are easy to make ahead and surprisingly delicate in flavour. If you are short of time, buy crackers or melba toasts, make the pâté and serve with a glass of Champagne.

Serves 8 (to share)

FOR THE MELBA TOASTS
8 slices white bread

FOR THE SMOKED MACKEREL PATE
250 g (9 oz) smoked mackerel fillet
1 bunch spring onions (scallions),
   thinly sliced
½ bunch dill, chopped
½ bunch chives, chopped
1 lemon, zested and juiced
100 g (3½ oz/generous ⅓ cup)
   crème fraiche
freshly cracked black pepper

To make the melba toasts, put the slices of bread under a medium grill and gently toast on both sides until light golden. Cut off the crusts and, using a long, sharp knife, split the slices in half, through the centre. Place the bread, untoasted-sides up, under a low grill until it curls into a crisp, golden shell.

To make the pâté, put the mackerel into a bowl with the spring onions, herbs, lemon zest and crème fraîche. Carefully fold the mixture together until fully mixed. Put the mixture in a food processor and pulse to the desired consistency.

Taste the pâté and season with black pepper and a squeeze of lemon juice. Serve with melba toasts.

DF

128

Mini Yorkshires

with Herb & Horseradish Mayonnaise

Home-made Yorkshires are so easy to make and nothing beats them, but if you wanted to make a lighter version you could easily serve the beef at room temperature in shop-bought tart cases with the herb and horseradish mayonnaise and fresh herbs.

Makes 12

FOR THE YORKSHIRE PUDDINGS
1 egg
85 g (2¾ oz/⅔ cup) plain
  (all-purpose) flour
85 ml (3¼ fl oz/generous ⅓ cup)
  water
rapeseed oil

FOR THE HERB AND HORSERADISH
  MAYONNAISE
100 ml (3½ fl oz/scant ½ cup)
  mayonnaise (good quality
  shop-bought)
2 tablespoons grated fresh
  horseradish
1 teaspoon English mustard
1 tablespoon finely chopped
  tarragon leaves1 tablespoon
  finely chopped chives
sea salt and freshly ground black
  pepper, to taste

FOR THE FILLING
300 g (10½ oz) piece of beef fillet

TO SERVE
12 tarragon leaves

Heat the oven to 200°C (400°F/gas 6).

To make the Yorkshire puddings, add the egg to the flour and mix in gently. Slowly add the water as you mix, stirring continuously to keep it smooth.

Put a few drops of oil into each hole of a 12-hole small muffin tray and put into the oven to heat. When the tray is hot, pour 2.5 cm (1 in) of mixture into each hole and put back in the oven. Cook for about 8–10 minutes until the mixture has puffed up and golden brown. Take out of the oven and cool on a cooling rack.

To make the herb and horseradish mayonnaise, mix all of the ingredients together.

Cook the fillet of beef rare, in a heavy frying pan over a medium-high heat for around 4–5 minutes on each side. Let rest for 5 minutes, slice thinly and warm the Yorkshire puddings.

Put a slice of the beef on a Yorkshire, add a dollop of herb horseradish mayonnaise and decorate with a leaf of tarragon. Or, for a lighter version, use shop-bought tart cases and serve the beef at room temperature with a dollop of the herb horseradish mayonnaise.

NF

Chorizo & Goat's Cheese Palmiers

Menu Planner
Elegant Brunch
(page 17)

These can be made in advance, rolled and kept in the freezer. The true cheats canapé with soft goat's cheese, smoky chorizo and buttery puff pastry. Quick, simple and stunning.

Serves 4–6

250 g (9 oz) ready rolled puff pastry sheets
3 tablespoons red pepper pesto or sundried tomato paste
50 g (2 oz) thinly sliced chorizo
150 g (5¼ oz) log goat's cheese, crumbled
1 egg, lightly beaten, to glaze
2 tablespoons nigella seeds

Heat the oven to 180°C (350°F/gas 4).

Unroll the puff pastry and spread the pesto or sundried tomato paste over the pastry, in an even layer, to the edges of the long ends and leaving a space of about 2 cm (1 in) at the edges of the short ends. Lay the slices of chorizo in lines lengthways, alternating with the goat's cheese.

Roll the two long sides up tightly to meet in the middle, turn over, and cut into 1 cm (½ in) wide palmiers, place cut-side down on a baking tray and press lightly to flatten slightly. Brush the palmiers all over (including the sides) with a little beaten egg, sprinkle over the nigella seeds and refrigerate for 30 minutes.

Bake for 12–15 minutes, or until crisp and golden-brown. Serve while still warm.

NF

Mini Meat Pies

with Bloody Mary Ketchup

Classic, crowd-pleasing meat pies with a bloody Mary ketchup that is spiked with vodka, horseradish and Tabasco. The perfect accompaniment!

Makes 12

1 onion, finely chopped

2 tablespoons vegetable oil, plus extra to grease

2 carrots, finely chopped

2 celery stalks, chopped

250 g (9 oz/2½ cups) chestnut (cremini) mushrooms, chopped

500 g (1 lb 2 oz) minced (ground) beef

1½ tablespoons plain (all-purpose) flour

500 ml (17 fl oz/2 cups) beef stock

1½ tablespoons tomato purée (paste)

dash of Worcestershire sauce

dash of soy sauce

2 bay leaves

2 sprigs thyme, leaves picked

sea salt and black pepper

320 g (11 oz) sheets puff pastry

FOR THE BLOODY MARY KETCHUP

200 ml (7 fl oz/scant 1 cup) good quality ketchup

3 tablespoons vodka

1 tablespoon Worcestershire sauce

1 teaspoon Tabasco sauce

1 tablespoon caster (superfine) sugar

1 tablespoon horseradish sauce

To make the filling, fry the onion and celery in the vegetable oil fover a medium heat for 8 minutes, add carrot and cook for 5 more minutes, then add the mushrooms and cook until soft and starting to brown. Turn up the heat and add the beef. Brown the meat, then sprinkle in the flour and stir to mix it in. Add the beef stock, tomato purée, Worcestershire and soy sauces, herbs, and season. Simmer, stirring regularly, until the gravy has thickened. Remove the pan from the heat and leave to cool.

Heat the oven to 180°C (350°F/gas 4).

Unroll the puff pastry and using a 9 cm (3½ in) cutter cut out 12 bases, then 12 tops with a 6 cm (2¼ in) cutter. Press the pastry circles down gently to make sure they fit the holes of the oiled muffin tin.

Add a heaped spoonful of filling to each pie case, leaving room for it to expand slightly. Brush the border of the filled pastry with water, then press the top piece on, creating a slight dome. Press the edges together and crimp if you like. Cut 2 small slits in the top of each pie and brush with beaten egg. Bake for 20–25 minutes, until crisp, golden and slightly risen.

Mix all the ingredients for the bloody Mary tomato ketchup in a bowl and serve alongside the meat pies.

NF

132

Gochujang Pork
with Quick Pickled Carrots

Gochujang is fermented chilli paste and has a relatively mild heat. Its mildness makes it a great all-rounder and in this pork dish served with bitter red leaves and pickled carrots it makes for a light, spicy and tangy dish.

Serves 8

1 onion, grated

1 thumb-sized piece fresh ginger root, peeled and grated

2 cloves garlic, crushed

3 tablespoons soy sauce

2 tablespoons brown sugar

2 teaspoons sesame oil

3 tablespoons gochujang

1 small pear, grated

2 tablespoons neutral-flavoured oil

500 g (1 lb 2 oz) pork tenderloin, fat removed and cut into small cubes

FOR THE QUICK PICKLED CARROTS

150 ml (5 fl oz/scant ⅔ cup) water

150 g (5 oz/generous ⅔ cup) caster (superfine) sugar

150 ml (5 fl oz/scant ⅔ cup) rice wine vinegar

pinch of sea salt

½ daikon radish, julienned

3 multicoloured carrots, julienned

TO SERVE

red leaves, such as raddichio

gochujang

To make the gochujang pork, combine all the marinade ingredients except the pear and the oil, put the pork in a bowl, pour the marinade over it, cover and leave to marinate for 30 minutes, or overnight.

To cook, heat the oil in a large, non-stick frying pan over a high heat and tip in the pork with the marinade. Cook at a high heat for 25 minutes and turn down until the pork is cooked and the sauce is syrupy. Add water if it thickens too much. Add the grated pear. Cook for another 5–7 minutes and take off the heat.

Meanwhile, for the pickle, combine the water, sugar and salt in a saucepan and boil on a medium heat until the sugar dissolves, around 3–4 minutes. Stir occasionally. Remove from the heat and leave to cool down.

Put the julienned radish and carrots into a sterilised pickling jar, pour over the brine, swirl and close the lid.

Leave the jar at room temperature for 3 to 4 hours then transfer to the refrigerator. Chill the pickles for 30 minutes to 1 hour before serving.

To serve, spread the radicchio leaves on a platter, top with the pork mixture and finish with a little of the pickle on each canapé, and some extra gochujang sauce on the side.

DF | **NF**

Lamb & Feta-stuffed Gozleme
with Muhammara

Originally from Turkey, this filled flatbread can be made with extra spinach, tomato and feta for vegetarians instead of using lamb. For a super-quick cheat's version, you can sandwich the filling in two tortilla wraps, cook on both sides and cut into bite-sized pieces and serve the muhammara alongside it.

Serves 8

7 g (¼ oz) sachet fast-action dried yeast
1 teaspoon sugar
250 g (9 oz/2 cups) strong white flour
generous pinch of sea salt
3 tablespoons olive oil

FOR THE FILLING
2 tablespoons olive oil
200 g (7 oz) minced (ground) lamb
2 aubergines (eggplants), finely chopped
1 onion, finely chopped
2 teaspoons ground coriander
2 teaspoons ground cumin
½ teaspoon chilli flakes
½ teaspoon ground cinnamon
200 g (7 oz) feta, crumbled
½ bunch spring onions (scallions), finely chopped
2 tablespoons pine nuts, toasted
sea salt and freshly ground black pepper

FOR THE MUHAMMARA
300 g (10½ oz) jar roasted red peppers, drained
4 tablespoons olive oil
100 g (3½ oz/1 cup) walnuts (toasted) a few reserved, to garnish
1 clove garlic, crushed
2 tablespoons tomato purée (paste)
100 g (3½ oz/1¼ cups) breadcrumbs
2 tablespoons pomegranate molasses
1 teaspoon chilli flakes
1 teaspoon date or maple syrup
1 teaspoon sumac
sea salt and freshly cracked black pepper

TO SERVE
reserved toasted walnuts, as above, chopped
extra-virgin olive oil
a handful of flat-leaf parsley leaves

134

Start by making the dough. Mix the yeast, sugar and 175 ml (6 fl oz/¾ cup) lukewarm water in a small bowl. Stir to dissolve the yeast, then set aside for 10 minutes, or until the liquid starts to froth. Mix the flour with the salt in a big bowl, pour in the yeasty mixture and the olive oil, and mix to a dough. Knead for 10 minutes, then put the dough in a lightly oiled bowl and cover with oiled cling film (plastic wrap) and leave somewhere warm to double in size. This should take about an hour.

Meanwhile, make the filling. Heat half the oil in a frying pan, add the mince and fry for 10 minutes, then the aubergine for another 10 minutes. Stir in the onion and spices and fry for a few more minutes, then turn off the heat and stir in the feta, spring onions, pine nuts and seasoning. Set aside to cool a little.

Divide the dough into 4. Working a piece at a time, roll out on a lightly floured surface to about 30 cm (12 in) long and 20 cm (8 in) wide, without the dough splitting. With one of the long edges of the pastry laid out in front of you, spoon a quarter of the filling on the bottom half, leaving a 2 cm (¾ in) border facing you and at each end. Fold the other half of the dough over the filling, folding in and pinching the edges to seal the mixture in. Heat a large frying pan over a high heat, brush the gozleme all over with oil and cook until golden on each side.

To make the muhammara, blend all the ingredients into a smooth paste in in a food processor then transfer it to a serving bowl.

Serve the muhammara drizzled with extra virgin olive oil and garnished with the reserved, chopped walnuts and fresh parsley leaves, alongside the gozleme.

135

Cheesy Pull-apart Bread

Menu Planner
Lazy Afternoon
(page 19)

This is a fantastic sharing show-stopper. Served alongside antipasti, it's perfect for the festive season.

Serves 8

250 ml (8½ fl oz/1 cup) milk
50 g (2 oz/scant ¼ cup) unsalted butter, chopped
1 tablespoon caster (superfine) sugar
2 teaspoons dried active yeast
485 g (10½ oz/scant 4 cups) strong white flour, plus extra for dusting
pinch of sea salt
2 eggs, whisked
4 sprigs thyme, leaves picked
3 sprigs rosemary, leaves picked and chopped
60 g (2 oz/generous ⅓ cup) sundried tomatoes, chopped
60 g (2 oz/½ cup) black olives, pitted and chopped
120 g (3½ oz) goat's cheese, crumbled
70 g (2¼ oz/½ cup) pine nuts, chopped
70 g (2½ oz) mixed herbs, such as chives, parsley and basil
60 g (2 oz) Parmesan (or vegetarian or vegan alternative), grated

Put the milk in a small saucepan and bring to a gentle simmer. Remove from the heat, add the chopped butter and the sugar and stir until the butter has melted. Allow to cool for at least 20 minutes before adding the yeast. Add the yeast, stir to combine and set aside for 5 minutes or until the surface is foamy.

Put the flour, salt, eggs and yeast mixture into the bowl of an electric mixer with a dough hook attached and beat for 5 minutes or until the dough is smooth, or alternatively mix togethet to form a dough, then knead on a floured work surface for 10 minutes. Transfer to a lightly greased bowl, cover with cling film (plastic wrap) and set aside for 1 hour or until doubled in size.

Heat the oven to 200°C (400°F/gas 6).

Roll out the dough on a lightly floured surface to a 32 cm × 35 cm (12¾ in × 14 in) rectangle. Sprinkle with the sundried tomatoes, olives, goat's cheese and pine nuts, a third of the mixed herbs and half of the Parmesan. Cut the dough in half lengthways.

Starting from the longer edge, roll each strip to enclose. Cut each roll into 16 rounds. Arrange the rounds in a lightly greased cake mould with the centre removed. Cover with cling film (plastic wrap) and set aside for 30 minutes or until doubled in size.

Remove the cling film (plastic wrap), top with a little more oil and bake for 20–22 minutes or until golden-brown and cooked through. Top with the remaining herbs and Parmesan and cook for 5 minutes. Serve in the centre of a board with antipasti.

The Antipasti Board

Serving Tips
Keep it simple and make it a selection of homemade and shop-bought items. The bread is the centrepiece, and all the other items around it could be a mixture to suit both vegetarians and meat-lovers.

Buy In
- three types of cured meat
- mini mozzarella balls with sundried tomatoes
- pesto
- two types of hard cheese – one vegan and a pecorino or nice piece of Parmesan
- marinated artichokes
- pickled peppers
- anchovy fillets
- fresh figs
- vegan, gluten-free flatbread option (depending on your guests, as the main bread is neither)
- a bowl of peppery rocket with a drizzle of balsamic vinegar

Cheesy Pull-Apart Bread with Antipasti Board, *pages 136-137*

Mezze Platter

All over the eastern Mediterranean and North Africa, mezze is an entire, unpretentious, sharing meal. It's designed for long visits, laughter and deep conversation. Having everything ready when your guests arrive is best as all these dishes can be served at room temperature.

Menu Planner
Pre-party
(page 18)

Serves 8

1 large cucumber, sliced into rounds

FOR THE HERBY LABNEH
500 g (1 lb 2 oz/2 cups) Greek yoghurt
sea salt
50 g (2 oz) mixed chopped herbs (mint, dill, parsley), plus extra to serve

FOR THE OLIVE & PISTACHIO TAPENADE
200 g (7 oz/1 cup) pitted green olives, rinsed, drained well
1 tablespoon capers, drained
1 garlic clove
1 tablespoon lemon juice
80 ml (3 fl oz/generous ⅓ cup) extra virgin olive oil
80 g (3 oz/generous ½ cup) toasted pistachios
¼ bunch flat-leaf parsley, leaves picked and chopped
freshly ground black pepper

First, make the labneh. Whisk yoghurt with 1 teaspoon salt. Pour into a colander lined with muslin set in a bowl, cover and refrigerate to drain overnight.

Stir the herbs through the labneh, form it into walnut-sized balls and set aside.

To make the tapenade, combine the olives, capers and garlic in a food processor and chop finely. With the motor running, gradually add the lemon juice and olive oil and process until blended. Transfer the tapenade to a bowl. Stir in the pistachios and parsley. Season to taste with pepper. (Can be made 1 day ahead. Cover and refrigerate.)

In a bowl, coat the labneh balls with a mix of mint, olive oil and seasoning. Flatten a ball lightly on top of the cucumber slices and serve.

Serving Tip
Buy in a selection of flatbreads, pickled vegetables, falafel, salads and dips and make two recipes from the book, such as the Halloumi Swirls with Skordalia on page 92.

Vegan Platter

A board filled with vibrant vegetables and dips free of meat, fish and dairy. These herby asparagus cigars are wrapped in crispy filo and have a fresh lemon zing – perfect centre stage on your vegan platter.

Menu Planner
Evening
Soirée
(page 18)

Serves 8

FOR THE ASPARAGUS FILO CIGARS
1 tablespoon finely chopped dill
1 tablespoon finely chopped parsley
1 tablespoon finely chopped chives
1 lemon, zested
8 sheets egg-free filo pastry, shop-bought
3 tablespoons olive oil
24 asparagus spears, tough ends trimmed
1 tablespoon sesame seeds

TO SERVE
vegan mayonnaise

Heat the oven to 200°C (400°F/gas 6).

Put the chopped dill, parsley, chives, and lemon zest in a small bowl, toss well to combine, and set aside. On a work surface, place one sheet of filo pastry and cover the remaining sheets with a clean, damp dish towel to keep them from drying out.

Brush the sheet of filo with a little olive oil, then sprinkle on some of the herb mixture. Using a sharp knife, cut the sheet of filo, vertically, into four strips. For each strip of filo place the end of one asparagus spear at the bottom edge, then tightly roll at a slight diagonal to enclose the length of the spear, and tuck in the end of the strip of filo at the tip of the asparagus. Brush with olive oil and place on a baking parchment-lined baking tray, then repeat for the remaining filo and asparagus.

Sprinkle with sesame seeds and bake for 18–20 minutes or until the filo is lightly browned and crisp.

Serving Tip
Buy in a selection of vegan dips, breads, falafel, vegan cheese, fruit and vegetables.

Other recipes from this book you could serve alongside it would be Crispy Potato Skins with Vegan Chive Dip, page 83 and Rainbow Fresh Spring Rolls with Spicy Peach Dressing, page 104.

| V | VG | DF | | NF |

Mexican Layer Dip

Menu Planner
Retro Games Night
(page 19)

A much lighter take on a 1980s classic. For an even lighter version use low-fat Greek yoghurt instead of the light crème fraîche. Adding charred corn shards at the end adds an extra layer of flavour and texture.

Serves 8

400 g (14 oz) tin black beans, drained and rinsed

200 g (7 oz) shop-bought guacamole

300 g (10½ oz) shop-bought fresh tomato salsa

300 g (10½ oz/generous ¾ cup) light crème fraîche

2 tablespoons taco seasoning

1 lime, juiced

100 g (3½ oz/¾ cup) grated mild cheddar

½ iceberg lettuce, thinly sliced

100 g (3½ oz/scant ⅔ cup) cherry tomatoes, halved

½ bunch spring onions (scallions), thinly sliced

50 g (2 oz/⅓ cup) black olives, pitted and roughly chopped

½ bunch coriander (cilantro), leaves picked

2 corn on the cob, kernels chopped lengthways into shards and charred (optional)

TO SERVE
tortilla (corn) chips

Spread the black beans in an even layer in the bottom of your serving platter. Spread the guacamole in an even layer on top of the bean layer. Top with a layer of salsa. In a separate, medium bowl, stir together the crème fraiche with the taco seasoning and lime juice. Spread in an even layer on top of the salsa.

Sprinkle the cheddar in an even layer over the crème fraiche layer. Top with thinly sliced lettuce, tomatoes, spring onions, black olives, coriander and corn shards.

Serve with corn chips.

Serving Tip
For a really retro experience, build all the layers in a glass serving dish so you can visibly see all the layers. This is also really fun made in individual glasses served with the chips on the side if you prefer not to share.

V   **GF**   **NF**

Roast Chicken Platter

Either roast your own chicken or buy a ready-cooked chicken and serve it on a platter, cut up or shredded with loads of other items to accompany it.

Serves 8

1 whole roasted chicken, shredded
1 head of kale, spines removed and blanched
2 avocados, thinly sliced
2 red onions, thinly sliced
350 g (12½ oz) jar roasted peppers, drained and thinly sliced
1 carrot, shredded
1 lemon, juiced
1 beetroot, peeled and shredded
50 g (2 oz/1 cup) mixed herbs, chopped

FOR THE SOUR CREAM DRESSING
200 g (7 oz/generous ¾ cup) sour cream
50 g (2 oz) pickled jalapeños, drained and chopped
1 tablespoon each chopped tarragon, dill and chives
3 tablespoons mayonnaise or crème fraîche
2 tablespoons white balsamic vinegar
1 garlic clove, crushed
sea salt, to taste

To make the dressing, combine the sour cream, chopped jalapeños, tarragon, dill, chives, mayonnaise or crème fraiche, vinegar, garlic, and salt in a small bowl, stirring with a whisk.

Arrange the kale on a platter with all the other ingredients and serve with the dressing alongside.

Serving Tip
Buy in bread rolls, cheeses and relishes to serve with this, and you could also make the Feta & Mint Hummus, page 89, and the Quail's Eggs with Avocado & Yuzu Whip, page 94.

GF

Cheesecake Bites

Menu Planner
Lazy Afternoon
(page 19)

Cheesecake Bites are a delicious bite-sized dessert that everyone loves. A rich creamy ricotta and cheesecake filling is nestled on an easy biscuit crust topped with berries, physalis and edible flowers, if using.

Makes 24

350 g (10½ oz) digestive biscuits (graham crackers)

150 g (5 oz/scant ⅔ cup) butter, melted

500 g (1 lb 2 oz/2 cups) ricotta

350 g (12 oz/generous 1⅓ cups) cream cheese

3 eggs

250 g (9 oz/generous 1 cup) golden caster sugar

1 tablespoon cornflour (cornstarch)

2 teaspoons vanilla paste

2–3 clementines, zested (reserve the fruit, to garnish)

1 lime, zested and juiced

150 ml (5 fl oz/scant ⅔ cup) double cream

TO SERVE

300 g (10½ oz/1⅓ cups) selection of small berries, to decorate

24 physallis, some halved, some with leaves intact

2 clementines (reserved, see above), segmented

Heat the oven to 160°C (320°F/gas 2). Line the base and sides of a 20 × 30 cm (8 × 12 in) shallow rectangular tin with baking parchment.

Put the biscuits into a food processor and whizz to very fine crumbs. Add the melted butter, pulsing, until well mixed. Tip the mixture into the tin and spread out evenly. Using the back of a metal spoon, press the mixture down firmly and bake for 10 minutes.

Clean the food processor bowl and add the ricotta, cream cheese, eggs, caster sugar, cornflour, vanilla paste, clementine rind and lime juice. Whizz until smooth, then pour the mixture into the cake tin. Bake in the oven for about 40 minutes until the mixture is lightly set all over. Take out of the oven and allow to cool to room temperature.

Whisk the cream to soft peaks. Spread thinly over the top of the cheesecake. Chill the cheesecake overnight.

Remove the cheesecake from the tin and peel the parchment from the sides. cut into 24 small squares. Arrange on a serving plate and top with the physallis, clementine pieces and berries.

V | | | | **NF**

Mini Cranberry Brownies

Menu Planner
Pre-party
(page 18)

This foolproof brownie recipe works beautifully with the tartness of the cranberries and the richness of the drizzled white chocolate. For extra crunch, add some chopped nuts to the mixture.

Makes 48 bite-sized pieces

400 g (14 oz) good quality milk chocolate

500 g (1 lb 2 oz/2 cups) unsalted butter

550 g (1 lb 4 oz/generous 2⅓ cups) caster sugar

6 eggs

100 g (3½ oz/generous ⅔ cup) good quality cocoa (unsweetened chocolate) powder

150 g (5 oz/scant 1¼ cups) plain (all-purpose) flour

2 teaspoons baking powder

pinch of sea salt

2 teaspoons vanilla paste

100 g (3½ oz/generous ⅔ cup) dried cranberries

TO SERVE
100 g (3½ oz) white chocolate, melted
dried rose petals

Preheat the oven to 170°C (340°F/gas 3).

Melt the chocolate and butter and set aside – you can do this either in a bain-marie or in the microwave, taking care to have it just melted, not cooking. Mix the eggs and sugar together. When the chocolate has cooled a bit, stir it into the egg mixture. Sift the flour, cocoa, and baking powder into the bowl, add the salt and vanilla paste and fold together with a spatula until smooth, then fold in the dried cranberries.

Line a 20 × 30 cm (8 × 12 in) baking tray with baking parchment and pour the mixture in. Bake for 25–30 minutes or until a skewer comes out clean from the edges – the middle can still be gooey (but it should not wobble when you shake the tin). Take it out of the oven and leave to cool.

Cut into 48 small squares, drizzle with melted white chocolate and scatter with dried rose petals.

V   **NF**

148

Coconut Macaroons

These gluten-free sweet treats are perfect for any occasion, and make a great 'to go' gift for guests in prettily tied paper bags. They are also handy to have around on your party prep day, for fancy snacking.

Makes 12–15

200 g (7 oz/scant 2¼ cups) desiccated (dried shredded) coconut

100 g (3½ oz/1 cup) ground almonds

397 g (14 oz) tin condensed milk

1 teaspoon vanilla extract

2 egg whites

a pinch of sea salt

TO SERVE

50 g (2 oz) chocolate, melted (optional)

12–15 glacé cherries (optional)

Heat the oven to 170°C (340°F/gas 5).

In a medium bowl, mix together the coconut, ground almonds, condensed milk and vanilla extract. Set aside. In the bowl of an electric mixer, beat the egg whites and salt until stiff peaks form. Use a large silicone spatula to fold the egg whites into the coconut mixture.

Roll the mixture into walnut size balls and place on a lined baking sheet. Bake in the oven for 15 minutes. Take out of the oven and leave to cool.

When the macaroons have cooled, drizzle with melted chocolate and add glacé cherries if you like.

| **V** | | **GF** | |

Vegan Truffles

Menu
Planner
Evening Soirée
(page 18)

Rich, decadent and luxurious, these vegan chocolate truffles have a nutty filling enclosed in luscious dark chocolate. The perfect ending to a great party.

Makes 18

100 g (3½ oz/1 cup) pecans
100 g (3½ oz/1 cup) walnuts
200 g (7 oz/2 cups) cooked
  chestnuts
40 g (1½ oz/⅓ cup) cocoa
  (unsweetened chocolate) powder
a pinch sea salt
½ teaspoon ground cinnamon
200 g (7 oz/generous 1 cup)
  medjool dates, pitted
3 tablespoons maple syrup
1 teaspoon good quality instant
  coffee
200 g (7 oz) dairy-free chocolate
1 teaspoon coconut oil

FOR THE COATING
sea salt
chopped nuts
cocoa nibs

Put the pecans, walnuts, chestnuts, cocoa powder, sea salt, ground cinnamon, pitted dates, maple syrup and instant coffee in a food processor or high-speed blender and process until it reaches the consistency of a thick paste/dough. Form the truffles into walnut-sized balls, place on a tray and put into the freezer for 30 minutes.

Melt the chocolate in a bain-marie or in a microwave and stir in the coconut oil.

Take the truffles out of the freezer and, one at a time, dip them into the melted chocolate. Use a fork to take them out, and tap away the excess chocolate. Lay them out on a sheet of baking parchment and top with either sea salt, chopped nuts, or cacao nibs, or a mixture of all three.

V | **VG** | **DF** | **GF**

Strawberries Two Ways

Menu Planner
Elegant Brunch
(page 18)
&
Retro Games Night
(page 19)

Truly the simplest sweet treat! So simple you will feel like a real cheat but when you place a platter filled with these strawberries on a table your guests will be amazed at how simple they are to make.

Chocolate Dipped
Topped with Sprinkles and Gold Leaf

Serves 8

200 g (7 oz) dark chocolate
16 fresh strawberries
hundreds and thousands,
  to decorate
gold leaf, to decorate (optional)

Gently melt the chocolate in a bain-marie. Pick up each strawberry by its leaves and dip it into the chocolate. Turn or swirl the strawberry to completely coat it in chocolate. Lift the strawberry out and shake gently to remove excess. Carefully lay the dipped strawberry on its side on a baking sheet. Repeat, dipping all the strawberries.

Allow half of the strawberries to set a little before starting the process of topping each tip with hundreds and thousands and gold leaf.

Coconut Cream Filled

Serves 8

16 fresh strawberries, core removed
2 × 400 ml (14 fl oz) coconut milk,
  chilled
1 teaspoon vanilla paste
1–2 tablespoons icing
  (confectioners') sugar
100 g (3½ oz) vegan dark chocolate
2 tablespoons shaved coconut,
  to garnish

For the coconut cream, open the cans and removed only the solid bit of the milk. Keep the liquid chilled and add to smoothies.

Combine coconut cream, vanilla and sugar until whisk until thick. Adjust sweetness if needed with additional sugar. Fill the pastry bag with the coconut cream mixture. Fill each strawberry with coconut cream.

When plating, squeeze a bit of coconut cream on the center of the plate for the middle strawberry. Then assemble remaining strawberries around it and drizzle with the melted chocolate and finish with shaved coconut of using.

| **V** | | | **GF** | **NF** |

152

Index

COCKTAILS & CANAPES

Acknowledgements

To my chief taster Matthew – thank you, as always.

Thank you to the wonderful Eve Marleau, Kate Pollard and the rest of the fabulous team at Hardie Grant – it truly is such a pleasure to work with a team of dedicated, passionate and creative like-minded group of people. To Sophie Yamamoto for the lovely design, and Jacqui Melville, the wonderfully talented photographer and scene setter; the warmest thank you. It truly does not feel like work.

About the Author

Kathy was born into a Greek family in Sydney, Australia but now resides in London, England with her English husband. With over ten years' experience in the food industry, she currently works as a food stylist, recipe writer, recipe tester and cookbook author.

Previously, she managed the Divertimenti Cookery School where she was inspired to embark into a cooking career and undertook the Leiths Diploma of Food and Wine where she qualified as a chef. Her food style is light, relaxed and accessible, drawing inspiration from her formal training at Leiths, Australian and Mediterranean heritage, and years of food industry experience across a range of roles, both organisational and practical.

Published in 2020 by Hardie Grant Books,
an imprint of Hardie Grant Publishing

Hardie Grant Books (London)
5th & 6th Floors
52–54 Southwark Street
London SE1 1UN

Hardie Grant Books (Melbourne)
Building 1, 658 Church Street
Richmond, Victoria 3121

hardiegrantbooks.com

British Library Cataloguing-in-Publication Data. A catalogue record for this book
is available from the British Library.

Cocktails and Canapes by Kathy Kordalis

ISBN: 978 1 78488 374 4

10 9 8 7 6 5 4 3 2 1

Publishing Director: Kate Pollard
Senior Editor: Eve Marleau
Design: Maru Studio
Photographer: Jacqui Melville
Props: Ginger Studios
Food Stylist: Kathy Kordalis
Editor: Gregor Shepherd
Proofreader: Susan Low
Indexer: Vanessa Bird

Colour reproduction by p2d
Printed and bound in China by Leo Paper Products Ltd.